WILSON
HENRY
IRVINE
and
The Poetry
of
Light

WILSON HENRY IRVINE

AND THE POETRY OF LIGHT

June 6-August 30, 1998

Florence Griswold Museum

Old Lyme, Connecticut

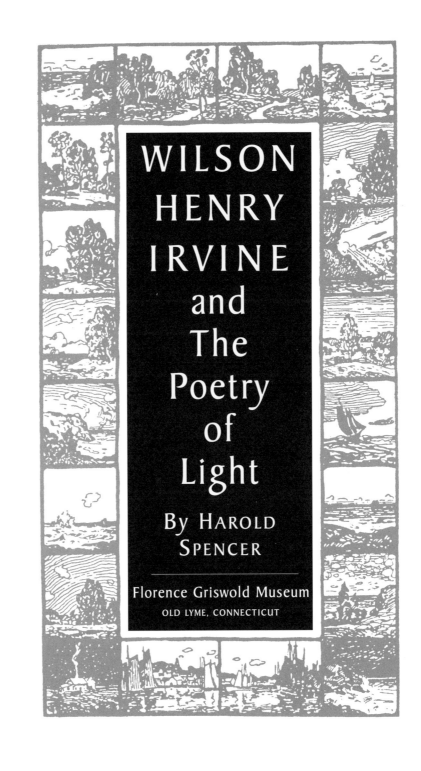

WILSON HENRY IRVINE and The Poetry of Light

By HAROLD SPENCER

Florence Griswold Museum

OLD LYME, CONNECTICUT

LENDERS TO THE EXHIBITION

Mr. and Mrs. Joel S. Dryer
Cynthia and John W. Everets
Florence Griswold Museum
The Geist Collection
Kirsten Halston
Mrs. Suzanne J. Harrington
Mrs. Marjorie Harshbarger
Illinois Historical Art Project
Joseph P. Irvine
Ms. Lydia Irvine Macdonald
    and Stewart Macdonald
Mr. and Mrs. Clement C. Moore
The Library of the National Museum
    of American Art
       and the National Portrait Gallery
Private Collections
Mr. and Mrs. Joseph Rhodes
The Rockford Art Museum
Smith College Museum of Art
Collection of the Union League Club
    of Chicago
The Wadsworth Atheneum
Mr. and Mrs. George M. Yeager

CREDITS

PHOTOGRAPHY

Joseph Szaszfai: Plates 1, 3, 4, 6, 8, 10, 12, 14, 18, 20; Figures 5, 20, 24 (top)

William Burt: Plates 13, 15; Figures 18, 24 (bottom), 26

Photography Collection, Lyme Historical Society: Page 8; Figures 15, 19, 28

CATALOGUE DESIGN
Tom Goddard

PRINTER
The Stinehour Press
Lunenburg, Vermont

TYPOGRAPHY
New Baskerville, Baker Signet

STOCK
Monadnock Dulcet, Lustro Dull

ISBN 1-880897-18-0
Copyright © 1998 Lyme Historical Society, Inc.
Printed by permission: Spencer, Harold.
"Wilson Henry Irvine and the Poetry of Light,"
Copyright © 1998 Harold Spencer.

Florence Griswold Museum
96 Lyme Street
Old Lyme, CT 06371

COVER: *Early Morning* (ca. 1912) detail,
by Wilson Henry Irvine.

CONTENTS

FOREWORD

UNDERPINNING the organization of this exhibition has been the conviction that the art of Wilson Henry Irvine (1869-1936) was in need of thorough reexamination. Although Irvine is chiefly remembered today as one of the American Impressionist painters active with the Lyme Art Colony in Old Lyme, Connecticut, much less understood is his prominent role in Chicago art circles prior to his move to Connecticut towards the end of World War I. The research accompanying this exhibition clarifies, for the first time, the contributions of those early years and examines the life and art of Wilson Henry Irvine in the broader context of both regions.

Irvine was a prolific artist and therein lies part of the problem of assessing his contribution to American art. The enormous volume of his art is matched by a wide range in its quality. Although recent gallery shows have reintroduced the public to aspects of Irvine's work, there has not been a thorough and systematic study of the artist. In 1994 the Florence Griswold Museum began to lay plans to assemble a selection of Irvine's finest works from public and private collections with the aim of organizing the first truly comprehensive retrospective exhibition devoted to this important American Impressionist.

To help us in this undertaking we turned to a scholar and colleague who was eminently qualified to make such a reappraisal — Dr. Harold Spencer, Emeritus Professor of Art History at The University of Connecticut, and the curator of the landmark *Connecticut and American Impressionism* exhibition at the University's William Benton Museum of Art. What we didn't know at the time was the extent to which Harold Spencer would discover invaluable resources that shed new light on

Irvine's career and, in the process, become completely absorbed in his subject. Relying on the use of the artist's diaries, sketchbooks, family correspondence, vital records, archival sources, and periodicals, together with the study of several hundred Irvine paintings, Professor Spencer has done a masterful job piecing together the strands of Irvine's life and drawing attention to the artist's considerable talents. All of us at the Florence Griswold Museum are indebted to our colleague and friend for his work as exhibition curator and author of the accompanying catalogue.

We are also deeply appreciative to members of the artist's family, to private collectors, and to public institutions, each of whom is listed on page 4, who have graciously shared their works with the Museum and without whose cooperation this exhibition would not be possible. Foremost among these lenders are George and Barbara Yeager who, upon receiving an Irvine as a wedding gift from the artist's family, assembled a collection over the succeeding years that is a definitive representation of the range and depth of Wilson Irvine's work. In fact the original impetus for *Wilson Henry Irvine and The Poetry of Light* stems from several leisurely and pleasant visits with the Yeagers. Several works from their collection form the cornerstone of this exhibition and we are indebted to George and Barbara Yeager for their generosity in sharing examples of their collection with the public so that we might gain a fuller understanding of Wilson Henry Irvine's contribution to American art.

JEFFREY W. ANDERSEN
Director

Wilson Henry Irvine
(1869-1936)

WILSON

HENRY

IRVINE

and

The Poetry

of Light

WILSON IRVINE is reported to have said that he liked to paint when there was "a kind of hazy beauty in the air."[1] This he surely did — and more — for he found each variation within the broad range of natural light and atmosphere, day to day, season to season, place to place, an invitation to grasp its specific character and set it down. A convincing sensation of light is so pervasive in Irvine's painting that one is inclined to conclude that the depiction of its fragile presence and the various moods its diversity could evoke was the underlying aim of this American impressionist. These luminosities infuse the settings in his landscape paintings — forest, pastorale, village, or harbor — with a poetic undertone that draws from the viewer the sentiments immanent in the artist's own affectionate response to the scene itself. Yet it is typical of his art that he also affirmed the solid substance of things even in the wash of light, a tendency not uncommon among the American impressionists, while his instinct for order tended to imbue his works with a firm compositional structure.

American impressionism, apart from those generic qualities which, stylistically, connect it with and distinguish it from the various forms of European impressionism, is often characterized by strong regional ties associated with art colonies centered around specific locales, each constituting a common painting ground for the artists and lending to the art produced there a shared sense of place. Such a colony developed in Connecticut, around Old Lyme, at the very end of the nineteenth century and during the early years of the twentieth, first with tonalist — "American Barbizon" — traits under the dominant presence of Henry Ward Ranger, then, after Childe Hassam's arrival in 1903, with a tenor increasingly impressionistic in mode.[2]

Although Illinois-born Wilson Henry Irvine (1869-1936) did not settle permanently in Connecticut until over a decade after Hassam's last summer in Old Lyme, he was attracted to the coastal and rural landscape of New England as early as 1905 or 1906. Subsequently, year after year, while still living in Chicago, he sketched and painted at various locations in the northeast, from the Maine coast to Cape Ann, from Monhegan Island to the Connecticut shore. By 1918 he had taken up permanent residence in Hamburg, a few miles north of Old Lyme, after having spent four summers painting in the area.[3] Over some twenty years, ever sensible of the transient nuances of light and weather, he tirelessly recorded the seasonal moods of the Connecticut landscape as well as scenes in other parts of the United States and, briefly, in Canada. Abroad, he found subjects in England, Wales, Scotland, France, and Spain. Although landscapes constitute the dominant genre, he also painted numerous still lifes, portraits, and figure compositions, producing an extensive body of work that represents an important contribution to the American impressionist movement, but one which has been too frequently overlooked despite his extensive exhibition record.

Irvine was already a mature painter when he settled in Connecticut after more than twenty-five years as an artist in Chicago. Thus, it is only in the contexts of both regions that his life and art can be properly examined. His Midwestern roots and the important role of the Midwest in the history of American impressionism, as well as his career in Connecticut, must each be accorded its appropriate consideration. Proper attention must also be given to the innovative phases of Irvine's art and their relationship to his perceptions of an artist's commitment to his craft. Although his work is rooted in a *plein air* impressionist approach to painting, his aquaprints of around 1927 and his prismatic paintings, which he began to exhibit in 1929, and some individual pieces of unique character, exemplify his inclination to explore beyond the normal boundaries of impressionism. Conservative in some respects, he was inventive and enterprising in others.

His career calls attention to two separate but related issues in the assessment of an artist's role and repu-

tation, as distinct from the quality of the art. The first of these has to do with the timing of the artist's appearance on the professional art scene as it bears upon matters of historical style and thematic choice. The second issue is both geographic and social in nature: where and under what circumstances does the artist's career begin and where and under what circumstances is it chiefly pursued. These two issues, examined in the context of Wilson Irvine's career, may account for his having received so little attention for one whose work has such high merit. In actual age, he was not a full generation younger than the first generation of American impressionists, but he is generally viewed as of the second generation. He spent over half of his career based in Chicago when the prime center for recognition was New York and came to the Old Lyme area after the colony there had passed the peak of the Hassam and Metcalf years. By this time, in those critical circles that shaped current opinion in the art world, and in the mainstream thrust of the younger generations of American artists, impressionism had been eclipsed by successive modernist styles, and interest in it lay dormant for more than a generation after Irvine's death — until attention to its historical significance and its regional manifestations led to a series of landmark exhibitions.[4] If there was a degree of skepticism over American impressionism's promotion by dealers in art, the prevailing sentiment favored a serious reexamination of a neglected body of work.

Emphasis on the derivative aspects of the American phase of international impressionism, repeatedly citing French origins, had largely ignored those continuities within it fostered by the American experience in an agrarian and village society which had rapidly evolved into an industrial and urban configuration following the Civil War. With the change came lingerings from the past, as rural places acquired some aura of sanctuary from the crowded cities and the smoke of factories. By and large, American impressionist landscape painting with its brightly keyed palette and its optimistic tenor was remarkably suited to play a role in this milieu. Rural, coastal, and village themes dominated, but while its *plein air* approach emphasized the transient moment and the immediate place, it was underlaid by veins of sentiment infused with values from that earlier era, values abundantly expressed in American prose and poetry and imbedded in a collective consciousness that held in reverence "the good old days." Recognition of this facet of American impressionism — not what it was as a vaguely defined style but what it *did*, what it communicated of nostalgia, sanctuary, respite, and renewal in accord with the times — gives cultural significance to its reassessment[5] and justifies a revival of interest in artists like Wilson Irvine, whose talents contributed to the body of work that defined the movement.

Since the market for Irvine's paintings was almost exclusively the private sector, the bulk of his art — and much of the best of it — generally went into private collections [Fig. 1], or stayed within the family, and thus for some time remained relatively unknown to a wider audience. It is also clear that he was exceptionally industrious and the sheer volume of his work — yet to be fully recorded — reveals a wide range of quality.

However, by assembling a retrospective exhibition of a selection of his finest works, attention can now be drawn more emphatically to Irvine's considerable talents, which would require no apology even in the presence of first-rate examples from the more famous American impressionists. A reassessment of his work has been long overdue.

FIGURE 1. Wilson Irvine, *Landscape, Lyme, Connecticut,* ca. 1914 [Cat. no. 10] (Smith College Museum of Art). This work was originally in the private collection of Mrs. Annie Coburn of Chicago.

THE EARLY YEARS

Wilson Irvine was born on February 28, 1869, near Byron, Illinois, in what is now Rockvale Township, Ogle County, where his family owned farmland along the picturesque Rock River. His great-grandfather, Alexander Irvine, a Methodist minister of Scottish birth, was one of the early settlers in the region, having moved there from Ontario province in Canada around 1836. Apparently his ministry did not impede his material enterprise: he is reported to have sold from "a shanty of logs" some goods which he had brought from Canada. His son, Joseph W. Irvine, the artist's grandfather, after years as a successful farmer on the family lands in Ogle County, became a prominent business executive in Rockford, Illinois, where he had resided since 1869[6], the year Wilson Irvine was born to Malinda (Underwood) and Edwin A. Irvine, Joseph's eldest son, still on the family farm. The artist's father had served in the Union army during the Civil War[7] and eventually became a railroad mail agent in Rockford.[8]

Apparently Irvine displayed an aptitude for drawing at an early age, for he is said to have been allowed to accompany his sister, Ila, to public school before he was old enough to enroll and there to occupy himself with drawing on his slate. Their mother reportedly encouraged both children to become involved in the arts, and subsequently Ila pursued a career as an actress and teacher of elocution and drama.[9] Irvine first attended school in Byron and is said to have worked as a newspaper reporter there when only about sixteen and later on in Rockford while still in high school, but whether these employments can be verified or related to his supposed work as a newspaper artist is still uncertain.[10] He graduated from Rockford's new Central High School in 1888.[11]

His earliest existing work may be a drawing, very likely a caricature, in his diary of that year. He must have regarded it very lightly, since diary entries are written directly on top of it.[12] His practice of keeping a journal now and then may have come from his father, who had kept a diary during the Civil War.[13] The diary of 1888 — a very small affair — had little space in it for more than six or eight short lines per day, so the entries are brief. Nevertheless, in its foreshortened way, it is a valuable source of information about the young man, revealing traits of character that mark his later self as well as providing a record of the intellectual and social life of a nineteen-year-old in a small Midwestern city of that era, and of his experience as he continued his education in Chicago.

To date, the first tangible evidence we have of Irvine's artistic activities comes from the beginning of 1888. In that year, one Liberty Walkup, together with his wife, established an art school in Rockford. Instruction in the use of the airbrush, which Walkup had invented and manufactured by 1883 [Fig. 2], was part of the curriculum.[14] There is no evidence that Irvine was a student at the Walkup's Illinois Art School, but in the diary of 1888 he states in the entry for January 2 that he had worked on the airbrush in the morning. The entry seems to imply that this was not the first occasion, so it is likely that Irvine had been using this new instrument at least as early as the latter part of 1887.[15] This places him among the first practitioners of a technique which would become an important feature of commercial and decorative art in the twentieth century. Within a few years his skills had apparently reached a professional level, for when he was married to Lydia C. Weyher of Lafayette, Indiana, on April 8, 1891, a Rockford newspaper reported that he was "a successful airbrush artist in Chicago."[16]

On January 3, 1888, the day following his reference to the airbrush, he wrote in his diary that he had worked that day on a landscape, "Morning in Holland." Obviously this was an imaginary scene or perhaps a copy of some picture of which he had a reproduction. Other than the obscured caricature and the reference to the airbrush, this is the only hint of "hands on" art activity in the 1888 diary.[17] The diary is silent on the subject of newspaper work.

Irvine's last few months in Rockford, as a senior in high school, were very busy but were shaping up, in his mother's view, as wanting focus. Only one month into 1888 he entered in his diary that she was of the opinion that he "must learn of the application of purposes." While he was engaged in studying history, literature, astronomy, and German, writing numerous papers on a wide variety of subjects from the Crimean War to the influence of age upon literature, reading novels, polit-

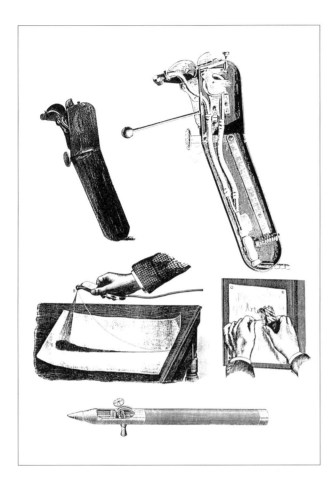

ical speeches, Shakespeare, Emerson, Darwin, and Madame De Staël, attending lectures and concerts, acting in the class play, going to church on most Sundays (denominations variable) and rating the sermons, he was also cramming in a considerable amount of socializing. There were dances, skating parties, rides in the country, and fishing in the Rock River come spring. He enjoyed the company of young ladies and found them fascinating: one "a good sound girl", another "dreamy" and "passionate", yet another "a saucy little flirt." He dated the latter the next evening. The ener-

gy that made him a profilic artist in his maturity was already apparent in his youth.

After graduation he embarked with a friend on a camping, rowing, and sailing trip in the Chain O'Lakes area in the northeastern corner of Illinois. They fished, swam, raced other boaters, and played chess in camp. Irvine did most of the cooking. The diary entries are brief, but they convey the sense that this was an idyllic interlude. He then set off for Chicago.

THE CHICAGO YEARS

Irvine's first months in Chicago were not devoted to art. According to his diary, he arrived there on July 16, 1888, and the following day was enrolled in a business school, learning shorthand. As the year progressed, his entries in the diary became less faithful. By November some of them were in shorthand, and by the middle of that month ceased altogether. It was August 11 before he noted anything related to art in that Midwestern metropolis: a visit to The Art Institute of Chicago, where he "enjoyed the pictures very much."

Precisely when Irvine began his attendance at evening classes in The Art Institute of Chicago has been variously reported, some sources stating that he started there as early as 1891, the year he was married,[18] but this is still unconfirmed. The records of The Art Institute of Chicago indicate that he was enrolled in the evening classes from 1895 to 1903: from 1895 to 1902 in the life class taught by Charles E. Boutwood, who had studied at the Royal Academy in London and in Paris with William Bouguereau and Robert Fleury; from 1902 to 1903 in the illustration class taught by Walter M. Clute, who had studied in New York at the Art Students League and in Paris with Jean

FIGURE 2. The top two illustrations are of the Rockford airbrush invented and manufactured by Liberty Walkup and which Irvine must have used as early as 1887. The bottom illustration is of the 1896 model of the Fountain Air Brush manufactured by Thayer & Chandler of Chicago. Irvine may have used this model later on in his commercial work in Chicago. Illustrations courtesy of Andy Penaluna, Swansea, Wales.

Constant and Jean-Paul Laurens.[19] Such formal training as Irvine received was thoroughly academic, concentrating on the human figure. His skills in landscape painting must have been largely self-taught.

Evening classes were the only practical alternatives for Irvine, a practical man with a growing family to support,[20] and apparently working by day at commercial art. To what purpose he was using his study of shorthand is not known.

Irvine's success with the new airbrush technology may have led to his employment by the Chicago Portrait Company shortly after it was established in 1893, since the airbrush was sometimes used in the finishing of portraits.[21] How long and in what capacities Irvine worked for the Chicago Portrait Company has yet to be firmly established, since the company has ceased to exist and its personnel records have not been located, but he is reported to have been an art manager and to have been with the firm until 1913.[22]

The Chicago Portrait Company was an extensive operation with representatives covering the country from the east coast to the Pacific northwest and as far south as Mississippi and Florida. It reported "steady patrons" in England, Canada, Nova Scotia, Cuba, Hawaii, and Mexico. The firm's salesmen solicited customers and gathered their photographs for reworking in the Chicago studios. By the turn of the century the company reported that there were some 2,000 salesmen on the road and 150 artists in Chicago engaged at rendering portraits in Conté crayon, Winsor & Newton colors, and pastels over "solarprint" photographs made from the originals supplied by the customers.[23] Since the airbrush was used in finishing some of these portraits, Irvine may have been employed initially in this capacity.

An amusing allusion to Irvine's service with the Chicago Portrait Company is recorded in the catalogue of a zany one-night exhibition held on February 12, 1898, by members of the Palette and Chisel Club of Chicago in which Irvine is identified as a "pupil of Acme Portrait Factory." He was represented in the show by a portrait, unidentified as to sitter.[24] This portrait was probably not a serious effort, because the exhibition was apparently a burlesque of a current show at The Art Institute of Chicago. It was also a burlesque in another sense. The title of the club's spoof — Salon de Refuse — was an irreverent and unserious reference to the famous, serious, and often revered French Salon des Refusés of 1863.

Farcical entertainment of this sort was not uncommon at the Palette and Chisel Club,[25] although the organization's primary mission was to provide quarters where its members could gather to draw, paint, and sculpt from a model [Fig. 3]. Irvine was one

FIGURE 3. Members of the Palette and Chisel Club in Lorado Taft's studio in Chicago. Irvine is the fourth figure in the back row to the right of the model. Courtesy of the Palette and Chisel Academy of Fine Arts, Chicago.

of the founding members, the club's treasurer in 1898, its president the following year. He was among those students in the evening classes at The Art Institute of Chicago who met to form the club in November of 1895, to further develop their skills at working from the live model, independent of instruction, as well as to gain for themselves an opportunity to work in color under natural light on the weekends, since most of the participants were, like Irvine, employed by day during the week. They soon began to meet on Sundays in the studio of sculptor Lorado Taft, who was sympathetic to their cause. After he moved to another studio, the club for some years occupied the vacated space.[26]

It was during this period, when he was engaged in commercial art, attending evening classes, and probably identified chiefly as a portrait artist[27] [Fig. 4], that he was also developing his skills as a landscape painter. By 1900 he was beginning to exhibit landscapes in group shows at The Art Institute of Chicago[28] and elsewhere in the area.

There is some indication of tonalist features in the early landscapes, and in a work like the somewhat decorative *Birches* of 1907 [Fig. 5], with its cadences of slender tree trunks among dark masses of foliage silhouetted against a pale sky, the emphasis is more on tonal contrasts and the well-defined patterns of trees and clouds than on transcribing the sensation of light.

From the standpoint of design alone, this painting seems close to some of the California painters of the period, like Arthur Mathews, Edgar Payne, Elmer and Marion Wachtel, William Wendt, and others, although the California "Eucalyptus School" to which the composition is more likely to be compared did not emerge until around 1915.[29]

Some of Irvine's landscapes which can be firmly dated to the first decade of the century, already show evidence of the summarizing methods of early impressionism, reductive in the transcription of the scene while sensitively recording the effects of natural light through tonal and chromatic contrasts. In Irvine's broadly rendered canvas, *Dawn*, of 1905 [Plate No. 17], a soft roseate tonality, keyed to the morning sky, tempers the masses of full-foliaged trees and penetrates the brighter patches of light in the foreground.[30] The brushwork, which in the foreground conveys an impressionistic freshness and lively texture, softens in the middle distance, emphasizing thus the receding space; and there, on a gentle slope, a shaft of light crosses a winding path, brightest at the point of crossing, a counterpoise that slows the spatial flow. It is a well-constructed composition.[31]

In a painting done in Brittany in 1908 [Plate no. 4] the French village subject, with its fishing boats and waterway, its simplification of architectural forms and,

FIGURE 5. Wilson Irvine, *Birches*, 1907 [Cat.no. 2] (Private Collection)

FIGURE 4. Wilson Irvine, *Alice*, ca. 1928 (detail). Irvine continued to paint portraits from time to time throughout his career, as in this later work. (Courtesy of Lydia Irvine Macdonald and Stewart Macdonald)

over all, a blonde tonality expressive of soft, filtered light recalls many French impressionist paintings of the early 1870s, especially similar motifs by Alfred Sisley and Camille Pissarro. In execution it is primarily a transcription of the scene just as it presented itself to the artist, a direct interpretation of substantial forms and surfaces rather than an exercise in style.

In a painting like *Cloud Shadows* [Cat. no. 33] the light touch of the surface texture is so dominant a microstructure as to be suggestive of a veil through which the image of the subject, hazy and soft-edged, is filtered back to the viewer. The effect is of a profound natural stillness out of which the warm glow of a light across a silvered stream and a line of rail fence in the shadows barely hint of human presence. In general, this particular work begs comparison with a series of views along the Seine by Claude Monet done around 1897.[32]

In *St. Ives, Cornwall* [Plate no. 2], a work from Irvine's 1923 trip abroad, the color texture asserts its presence in a much more agitated way, joining with the swaying masts, the ruffled surface of the harbor, and the swarming of gulls to evoke the constant motion, rocking and swooping — even the sounds — in the busy fishing port. Here, and in other instances, there seems to be a relationship between his technical procedure and the nature and meaning of his subject, as if the painting's style were to some degree the product of its theme.

It is likely that Irvine's introduction to impressionism derived from his study of works that came to Chicago in the early 1890s as well as from the changes that were taking place in the region's art circles in the years around the turn of the century.

The World's Columbian Exposition of 1893 had brought to Chicago some of the finest examples of European and American impressionism,[33] pictures to whet the ambitions of the young artist, whose response to the experience must have been reinforced by his acquaintance with writer Hamlin Garland, a fellow member of The Cliff Dwellers, a prominent Chicago cultural organization that brought together professional artists, architects, writers, musicians, and patrons of the arts[34] [Fig. 6].

The Chicago art scene, following the World's Columbian Exposition, was abuzz with talk of impressionism, with its "prevalence of blue or purple shadows, and…abundance of dazzling sunlight effects" which Hamlin Garland cited in his essay "Impressionism" from his little volume *Crumbling Idols*, published in 1894.[35] The essay was an enthusiastic endorsement of impressionism, which he viewed as an international phenomenon that was bringing fresh vitality to the art of painting and to landscape painting in particular. Garland's essay, inspired by the impressionist works he had seen at the exposition, now occupies an important place in the literature of the American phase of the movement. Since he and Irvine were obviously well acquainted — Irvine having served often on The Cliff Dwellers' Art Committee and with Garland, the club's long-time president, on the Board of Directors[36] — there must have been some dialogue now and then on the merits of impressionist painting.

As a rising literary figure, Garland's preeminence in the city's cultural circles would surely have recommended his opinions to the ambitious Irvine. Sometime around 1915-1916 Irvine painted *Garland's Town*, probably a view of West Salem, Wisconsin, near Garland's birthplace, and where the writer had settled his parents. The painting may have been a tribute to Garland's long tenure as president of The Cliff

Dwellers, an office he relinquished to banker and art patron Charles Hutchinson in 1915.

Garland had come to Chicago from Boston when the exposition was about to open and "the newly-acquired studios were swarming with eager and aspiring young artists." He was convinced that Chicago would become "a publishing center and a literary marketplace second only to New York...more progressive than Boston, and more American than Manhattan."[37] He stayed for nearly a quarter of a century before returning east, having been an eloquent spokesman for an impressionism carried forward by those he called "veritists" — artists who looked directly at the immediate natural world rather than through the filter of the older established historical styles. His observation that impressionist painting was, for this reason, essentially *local* highlights one aspect of American impressionism which fostered its regionalism — its linkage to the specifics of place.

"They therefore strive to represent in color an instantaneous effect of light and shade as presented by nature, and they work in the open air necessarily," he wrote. "They are concerned with atmosphere always. They know that the landscape is never twice alike. Every degree of progress of the sun makes a new picture... It will thus be seen that these men are veritists in the best sense of the word. They are referring constantly to nature... They do not paint leaves, they paint masses of color; they paint the *effect* of leaves upon the eye."[38] The convictions set forth in Garland's essay read like a credo for Irvine's approach to the art of painting. It is not at all far-fetched to conclude that the writer's words may have become the painter's early and persistent guides.

During the years following the exposition a number of artists in the Midwest were beginning to aban-

don earlier Munich and Barbizon manners in favor of the brighter key of the impressionist palette. Among these were several painters who flocked to the picturesque hill-country of southern Indiana around Brown County,[39] a remote area accessible only by horsedrawn vehicles until the Illinois Central Railroad ran a line across the northwest corner of the county in 1905.[40]

In 1907, upon the recommendation of painter Adolph Shulz (who, together with Theodore C. Steele, became a central figure in the Indiana group) Wilson Irvine spent two weeks sketching in Brown County with fellow artists Louis O. Griffith and Harry L. Engle. The three had been students in the same evening classes at The Art Institute of Chicago. Although Shulz later reported that "they were delighted with the scenery and the people,"[41] there is no evidence that Irvine ever returned to this Indiana region. Therefore, assertions that he was involved in the estab-

FIGURE 6. Gathering at the "Khiva," the penthouse quarters of the Cliff Dwellers club atop Orchestra Hall, South Michigan Avenue, Chicago. Irvine is the second from the right at the table, Loredo Taft is second from the left. Courtesy The Cliff Dwellers, Chicago.

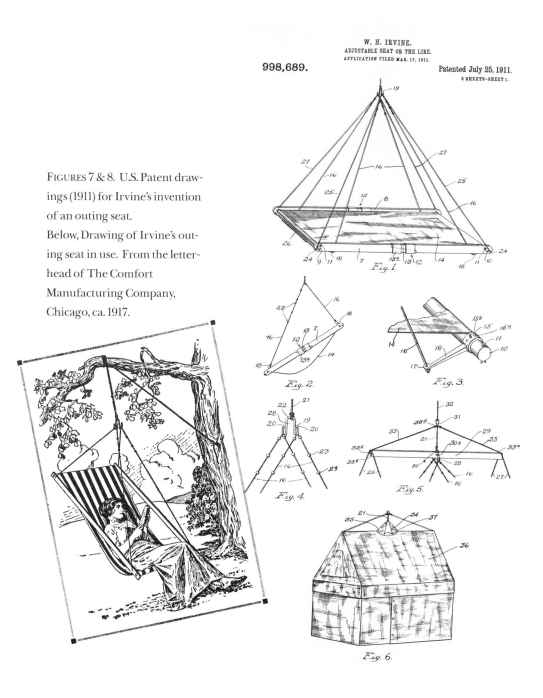

FIGURES 7 & 8. U.S. Patent drawings (1911) for Irvine's invention of an outing seat.
Below, Drawing of Irvine's outing seat in use. From the letterhead of The Comfort Manufacturing Company, Chicago, ca. 1917.

lishment of the Brown County art colony are clearly misleading.[42] His friend Griffith, however, did become active in the "Hoosier" group.

Although Irvine was not directly involved in the "Hoosier" school, with its close ties to Indianapolis and Brown County, its prominent place in the development of impressionist aesthetics in the "Middle Border," as Garland dubbed the Midwest,[43] was surely not lost on Wilson Irvine, who was personally acquainted with some of the artists associated with the Indiana group. Moreover, Garland's high regard for these artists, especially Theodore C. Steele,[44] was well known. During the 1890s Steele's example may have had some influence on the young Irvine, who would have been able to see the former's work at the World's Columbian Exposition. In 1894 the Indiana group exhibited in Chicago at Lorado Taft's studio and in 1896 Steele was one of the founding members of the Society of Western Artists[45] of which Irvine became a member.

Irvine, meanwhile, once he began his career as a landscape painter around the turn of the century, was increasingly on a quest for painting grounds outside the Midwest. However much the Indiana movement may have reinforced his impressionist bent, his work seems generally to have drawn him more and more towards the east coast and the New England impressionists.

During these Chicago years Irvine's native inventiveness emerged in a curious way: in 1911 he was granted a patent for an ingenious "outing seat" [Figs. 7 & 8] which could be suspended from an overhead support and could also be adjusted to serve as a sleeping cot with a tentlike cover. Its design would have done credit to a ship's rigger.[46] This inventive turn of mind surfaced again during World War I when he presented to the United States government a plan for a motor-driven shield for infantry. It was rejected by the War Department.[47]

As Wilson Irvine became more and more engaged in landscape painting, he traveled frequently in search of new painting sites. His constant pursuit of fresh subjects signals a degree of innate restless energy, a thirst for new scenes the likes of which he had not painted before. The intense focus upon the immediate subject, which Garland had cited as a characteristic of his "veritist" painters seems, in Irvine's case, to have demanded a constant quest after fresh motifs in new locales.

Titles of works he showed during the Chicago years place him at one time or another in Montana, Michigan, Wisconsin, Maine, Massachusetts, and Connecticut. In 1908 he traveled to France, visited Paris, and painted in Brittany, at St. Malo, Pont-Aven, Trémalo, and Concarneau. Notes in one of his sketchbooks place him in August of 1909 in Pittsburgh, Pennsylvania, where he visited the Carnegie Institute and jotted down brief comments on the works he saw: principally loans, he noted. Jean François Millet, Gari Melchers, Théodore Rousseau, Charles H. Davis, and Alexander Wyant were among those whose works he especially liked. A John Constable displayed a "modern idea of light," a Lillian Genth nude was "a wonder," he guessed Frederick Waugh "knew water," and Hassam's *Old Lyme Church* was "one of the best pictures by an American." He would continue to record his reactions to works by other artists in the journals he kept on trips to Europe later on.

His travels to New England began around 1905 or 1906 and included — sometime between 1905 and 1910 — a walking trip in mid-October from Ashland, New Hampshire, along Squam Lakes towards Sandwich. He had come up to Ashland from Boston, probably by

FIGURE 9. Irvine painting by the harbor, Gloucester, Massachusetts, probably between 1905 and 1910. Courtesy Lydia Irvine Macdonald and Stewart Macdonald.

train, after having spent some time on Cape Ann [Fig. 9]. He recorded, with glowing descriptions of the landscape, a portion of this experience in one of his sketchbooks.[48] In the journal he kept on his 1923 trip abroad he mentioned Oregon and the Dakotas in such a way as to suggest that he had visited those states as well. Apparently, for this landscape painter based in Chicago, it was necessary to get out of the city and off the local prairies.

There were painting sites, however, at no great distance from Chicago. During the summer months the Palette and Chisel Club operated a camp at Fox Lake [Fig. 10] about fifty miles north of the city. Here members could gather and spend their time painting and sketching in the out-of-doors.[49] Irvine was among those who frequented the Fox Lake site, an area which he had known during the Rockford years.[50] In the summer of 1913 Irvine and three of his colleagues from the club were reported to have "opened a new sketching ground at Buchanan, Michigan,"[51] which lies in a hilly section in the extreme southwestern corner of that state. Irvine was evidently a peripatetic painter.

By 1911 he had become an important presence in Chicago art circles. He was among the first directors of the Artists' Guild, established in 1910, for the purpose of encouraging higher standards of craftsmanship, to promote the sale of art, and to maintain a permanent salesroom as well as a bureau of information for artists and clients. It was the predecessor to the Arts Club, formed in 1916, of which Irvine was also a member. Like The Cliff Dwellers, it brought together artists and patrons of the arts. In 1911 Irvine became president of the Chicago Society of Artists. He soon was named chairman of the Chicago Commission for the Encouragement of Local Art, created in 1915 by the mayor's office to select and purchase paintings for the use of the city, a position which carried with it considerable power in that it was an ongoing purchasing agency. Irvine held the position until 1918, when he moved east. He was also president of the Chicago Water Color Club, which was active at least from 1908 to 1914, and The Chicago Society of Etchers named him an honorary member.[52] Meanwhile he was beginning to exhibit extensively and to win awards.

Commencing in 1900, Irvine showed in forty-one exhibitions at The Art Institute of Chicago, the last in 1926, except for a posthumous showing in 1939. In 1903 he was awarded First Prize in the Palette and

FIGURE 10. Palette and Chisel Club gathering at Fox Lake, Illinois. Irvine is in the back, to the right of the man with the upraised arm. Courtesy Palette and Chisel Academy of Fine Arts.

Chisel Club exhibition. In the Chicago and Vicinity exhibitions held at The Art Institute of Chicago, Irvine was awarded the Municipal Art League Purchase Prize in 1911, the Clyde M. Carr Prize in 1915, the Chicago Society of Artists Silver Medal, the Municipal Art League Prize, and the Palette and Chisel Club Prize in 1916, and in 1917 the Mrs. William Frederick Grower Prize. In 1912 he won the Martin B. Cahn Prize in the American Annual at The Art Institute of Chicago and in 1915 a Silver Medal at the Panama-Pacific Exposition in San Francisco. In 1916 he was honored with a solo exhibition of twenty-seven paintings at The Art Institute of Chicago, featuring subjects from his sojourns in New England.

He showed frequently with the Society of Western Artists and served as a juror for exhibitions at The Art Institute of Chicago and the Pennsylvania Academy of Fine Arts. He exhibited at the Carnegie Institute annual in 1908, 1909, 1911, and 1914; at the Corcoran Gallery of Art biennial in 1912, 1916, and 1926; at the Pennsylvania Academy of Fine Arts annual in 1909, 1910, 1913, 1914, 1916, 1917, 1921, and 1925; at the National Academy of Design in 1915, 1917, and each year from 1921 through 1936; at the Toledo Museum of Art in 1915 and 1916, and at several other venues while still based in Chicago.

In 1916 a review of Irvine's one-man exhibition at The Art Institute of Chicago remarked that "Mr Irvine's facility has grown so rapidly that it is difficult to keep pace with his advance. He is faithful to landscape, and in his sojourn in New England seems to have acquired a richer color texture, a surface quality, and a finish such as is always gratifying…" The reviewer saw in these works "decisive character" and "dignity."[53] A review of his exhibition of New England landscapes at O'Brien's galleries in Chicago during

December of 1918 was chatty and enthusiastic, finding that "the place has been sought and found" and that the paintings had "both poetry and imagination."[54]

Around this time Irvine belonged to a small circle of seven artists called "Painter Friends" comprised of George M. Bruestle, George H. Macrum, Edward C. Volkert, and Guy C. Wiggins, who listed their addresses as New York; Carl J. Nordell of Boston; and Robert H. Nisbet of South Kent, Connecticut. In 1917 Irvine, still listing a Chicago address, was the sole member west of Manhattan,[55] but by then he was obviously preparing for the move east.

The period immediately preceding his residence in Connecticut — that is, from around 1914 to 1918 — was an especially productive time for Irvine [Fig. 11]. He was spending summers painting in the northeast and some of his finest works were products of that experience. Three canvases from this period could be viewed, collectively, as a paradigm of a rural New England celebrated by American writers and painters, an image as stubborn in popular perceptions as the stony soil that underlies the scenes.

In *The Old Homestead* [Plate no. 5] a substantial Connecticut farmhouse, shaded by tall elms, is viewed from across a country road that runs between low stone walls. Architecture and setting are joined in complete harmony, weaving an eloquent, introspective image of quietude and rural sanctuary. In contrast, *Autumn* [Fig. 12] opens outwards onto a light-struck, rocky hillside crowned by trees, some in fall colors, others still green. A low stone wall, that omnipresent New England landmark, extends from the lower right diagonally up the slope to the left, adding its irregular line to the cadences of tree trunks, corn shocks, rail fencing, and scattered boulders and ledge. Although consummately generic in cataloguing the typical,

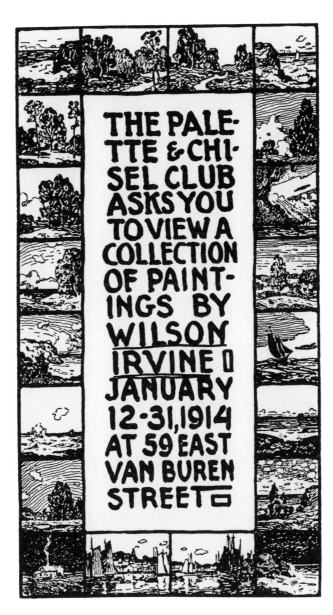

THE PALETTE & CHISEL CLUB ASKS YOU TO VIEW A COLLECTION OF PAINTINGS BY WILSON IRVINE □ JANUARY 12-31, 1914 AT 59 EAST VAN BUREN STREET □

FIGURE 11. Invitation to Irvine's solo exhibition at the Palette and Chisel Club in 1914. This show featured work from his earlier trips to New England. It is likely that Irvine himself created the invitation which incorporates, in the borders, drawings after his paintings, some of which have been identified. The third work from the left on the bottom row is *Evening in the Harbor* [Plate no. 16]. Courtesy Palette and Chisel Academy of Fine Arts.

Autumn is also thoroughly specific as to sense of place. *Candlewood Ledge* [Plate no. 6], awash in soft, clear, summer light, is a sweeping view across the exposed ledge to Hamburg Cove in the valley below and beyond this,

FIGURE 12. Wilson Irvine, *Autumn*, ca. 1914. Oil on canvas, 32 1/4 x 40 1/4 inches. The Art Institute of Chicago. Gift of Friends of American Art, 1915.

over gently rolling fields, to wooded hills in the distance. Almost panoramic, it maps this Connecticut locale with obvious affection for a landscape in which the human presence and the natural world seem to coexist in balanced accord. This triad of paintings, executed with spirited assurance, represents an exceptionally apt distillation of an ambience that can still be found along the back roads of New England. The summers spent near Old Lyme had convinced the artist that this was the milieu for steady painting.

Connecticut Landscape [Plate no. 7], like *Candlewood Ledge*, overlooks a valley with distant hills on the horizon, but there is a distinct difference in mood, light, and the treatment of space. *Connecticut Landscape* is more tonal, muted in color, and a hazy atmosphere softens the distance. The valley floor is more remote than in *Candlewood Ledge* and set off from the foreground by a high ledge and a repoussoir of trees. The river is a thin, pale ribbon in the distance. The

ruggedness of the foreground and the life cycle implicit in the trees atop the ledge recall an earlier romantic mood in American painting.

Although he had settled permanently in Connecticut by 1918,[56] Irvine maintained his strong connections with Chicago and with friends in Rockford. He listed Chicago addresses when he exhibited in group shows at The Art Institute of Chicago from 1918 through 1921. He continued to participate in annual exhibitions at that institution through 1926 and his main dealer seems to have been Carson, Pirie, Scott and Company Galleries until the mid-1920s. Moreover, since his two sons and daughter had established residences in the Midwest, there were personal as well as professional ties to draw him back to his native region. But it is obvious, from the titles of the works he exhibited during the Chicago years, that the varied landscape of the northeastern United States was increasingly the subject of choice. And, after the sampling of Brittany in 1908, New England may have had some additional appeal by being closer to Europe. Precisely why he should choose to settle near Old Lyme is, to date, undocumented, but there are several factors that may have some bearing on the decision.

THE MOVE TO CONNECTICUT

In December of 1916, The Art Institute of Chicago announced the forthcoming solo exhibition by Wilson Irvine, indicating that some twenty-five works would be shown "executed in the environs of Hamburg, Connecticut, where he has occupied a studio for the last three summers."[57] Regardless of when Irvine first visited the area where he finally settled, it is therefore clear that he considered it a likely place at least as early as the summer of 1914, part of which he spent on Monhegan Island [Plate no. 18] off the Maine coast.[58] This was also the year the Lyme Art Association was organized. At that time the art colony at Old Lyme was basking in the afterglow of the Childe Hassam and Willard Metcalf summers at the Griswold House — Hassam from 1903 to around 1907 and Metcalf from 1905 to 1907. After their departure both had continued for a time to exhibit with the Old Lyme artists, Metcalf until 1909 and Hassam until 1912.[59] It is reasonable to assume that Wilson Irvine may have been drawn to Hamburg partly by virtue of its proximity to a celebrated art colony committed to an impressionist point of view and stamped with the imprimatur of two of the nation's foremost painters. Of course, the rural and small village charms of the surroundings themselves that had so attracted Henry Ward Ranger in 1899 lay at the core of the colony's existence, and Irvine had a good eye for areas abounding in appealing landscape subjects. He had also demonstrated, in Chicago, his involvement in the society of fellow artists, so, in this respect, too, the Lyme colony may have had a special appeal. Other artists who lived in the Hamburg area included Guy Wiggins, George M. Bruestle, and Robert and Bessie Vonnoh.

It is uncertain whether his close friendship with the Vonnohs played a role in his choice of the Old Lyme area as a permanent residence. In Chicago, as a member of the Little Room, Irvine may have met painter Robert Vonnoh's future wife, sculptor Bessie Potter, since her studio was one of the meeting places for the group. Furthermore, Hamlin Garland was already acquainted with Vonnoh before coming to Chicago, and it may have been through the former that Irvine met his future neighbor. By the time Irvine began spending summers in Hamburg, the Vonnohs

had already, for several years, been maintaining a summer residence nearby [Fig. 14]. Their place was the subject of a canvas by Irvine, done around 1916, and shown that year in his solo exhibition at The Art Institute of Chicago.

FIGURE 14. Wilson Irvine, *Abandoned*, ca. 1916 (Cat. no. 13). The subject is the Vonnoh house, but whether it is the painting exhibited in Chicago in 1916 is uncertain. (Courtesy of Mr. and Mrs. George M. Yeager)

Irvine must also have viewed the move east as beneficial to his career. He was beginning to show in eastern exhibitions, at the Carnegie Institute, the Pennsylvania Academy of Fine Arts, the Corcoran Gallery of Art, and the National Academy of Design. His focus was shifting eastward despite his strong native attachment to the Midwest. He had enjoyed a good market for his painting in the Chicago area and would continue to do so after his move to Connecticut, but an eastern base would offer fresh opportunities for expanding his clientele. He was, after all, a professional artist living by the sales of his art.

Town records in Lyme indicate that Irvine

FIGURE 15. "Brooksound," the Irvine home in Hamburg.

FIGURE 16. Wilson Irvine and his wife, Lydia Weyher Irvine, in the late 1920s.

acquired in 1918 "Brooksound," the hillside property in Hamburg which he was to make his home for the remainder of his life [Fig. 15]. There was work to be done on it, including the addition of a studio, but the site was — and still is — a charming spot. Having discovered the place on one of his earlier explorations of the area, the story goes that he returned to look at it several times and "unwittingly caused the price to double."[60]

Irvine first exhibited with the Old Lyme artists in 1914, and continued to show with them for the remainder of his life. The first exhibition of the Old Lyme group had been held in 1902 at the Phoebe Griffin Noyes Library, Old Lyme, and continued to be held there until 1921, seven years after the Lyme Art Association was formed. In 1921 the present Lyme Art Association gallery, designed by Charles Platt, was inaugurated and subsequent exhibitions have been mounted there. In the inaugural year of the new gallery Irvine was awarded the W.S. Eaton Purchase Prize at the Lyme Art Association exhibition, and in 1934 the Mr. and Mrs. William O. Goodman Prize. The records show that he was an active member of the organization, displaying the kind of involvement he had so conspicuously demonstrated in Chicago.

In 1922 Irvine's exhibition of twenty-five paintings at Carson, Pirie, Scott and Company galleries in Chicago was of New England subjects. The following year he would go farther afield.

PAINTING ABROAD: GREAT BRITAIN AND FRANCE

The journals Irvine kept on his trips abroad in 1923 and 1929 provide a vivid account of the artist's day to day activities. As such, they provide an intimate view of the artist, his attitudes and temperament, his working habits and problems as a *plein air* painter, his on-the-spot relationships with others, his impressions of other artists' works, his responses to his surroundings, and his interests outside of art.

On February 3, 1923, Irvine and his wife [Fig. 16] sailed from New York.[61] On the eve of departure, Irvine had dined with Robert Vonnoh at the Salmagundi Club. The North Atlantic passage was particularly rough. The ship rolled and pitched heavily in a severe storm, tossing furniture about and throwing passengers out of their bunks. Irvine, an avid chess-player[62] [Fig. 17], was often unable to keep the pieces on the board but won enough games in calmer moments to give him some satisfaction. He found the wild ocean visually "wonderful" and "stunning," but he was happy enough, Lydia happier, to disembark in Plymouth, England, on February 11, which had dawned fine and clear. They went immediately up to London and the next day purchased a second-hand Ford touring car for the journey to their first destination, St. Ives, on the coast of Cornwall, and to points beyond. In London they visited the Tate Gallery where Irvine momentarily set aside his impressionist predilections.

"A stunning French room. Gauguin's long picture, a decoration, proves him one of the greatest of modern masters. The scheme of orange is lovely." So wrote Irvine of Paul Gauguin's *Faa Iheihe* which he had seen that day at the Tate Gallery.[63] Of all the other works he must have viewed in the French section, or elsewhere in the museum, he mentioned only Gauguin's piece in his journal. One would have expected some mention of Turner.

Without placing exceptional emphasis on his enthusiasm for this work by Gauguin, the implications of his comment are worth noting. The obvious anti-impressionism of Gauguin's painting was quite overridden by Irvine's sympathetic response to its glowing color and its decorative qualities. Apparently, his reaction to the painting had little to do with its exotic subject, but, instead, was rooted in the purely sensuous elements of color and form. In assessing this episode we might conclude that Irvine's response to the work was indicative of his own sensitivity to color as an interpretive agent, of his consciousness of underlying abstract schema in composing a picture, and, perhaps, of a growing flexibility in his aesthetic point of view. While not without firm convictions, Irvine was by no means unimpressionable.

Indeed, he seems never to have been uncritical of his own work or — some time later — the direction it had taken, revealing a vein of humbleness, even self-doubt.[64] His receptiveness with respect to Gauguin is consistent with that innovative tendency which surfaced in his own work from time to time, and may be symptomatic of the impulses which would lead him to experiments, such as his aquaprints of a few years later and his prismatic paintings of the late 1920s.

Upon reaching St. Ives on February 20, Irvine promptly found a studio flat on the wharf, "hardly more than a barn" but roomy and with a good north light. With some irony he remarked its airiness. But he soon discovered that the unpredictable weather on the Cornish coast at that time of the year was a force to contend with if you were a *plein air* painter. The draughty shelter of the studio served him well on many occasions.

"Rush out, set my stuff up and start, then gray, a cloud and a drop of rain, then a down pour, beat it and dam[n] the weather." This on March 1, and the weather continued its fitful ways week after week. But they remained in St. Ives, except for a two-week spell in a cottage at nearby Zennor, until June 1, when they moved on to Clovelly for a week before driving north into Wales. Still, despite the Cornish climate, Irvine kept busy at his painting, coping with "rubbernecks" and other nuisances, and working inside when it was impossible out-of-doors.

FIGURE 17. Irvine (left) playing chess at the Cliff Dwellers club with fellow artist Edgar Cameron. Courtesy The Cliff Dwellers.

When he first arrived at St. Ives and was painting on a Sunday, he was informed that some of the villagers had once thrown an artist into the harbor for that transgression. Hence, though some perfect weather turned up now and then of a Sunday, he grumpily refrained from setting up his easel on that particular day. On March 30 he noted: "Good Friday and of course they would line you up against the wall if one worked today, so I hypocritically kept the day — by working inside."

Although plagued by fickle skies throughout this period abroad he worked ardently and regularly at his painting, starting or completing some ninety or more works in Cornwall, Wales, Outer Hebrides, and Brittany, about one work every three days. It was a productive trip and the results were evident in his exhibitions upon his return home. One especially fine painting from among several such done in Cornwall is *The Quay, St. Ives* [Cat. no. 26] which records one of the better days of Cornish weather and which, like his earlier 1908 Breton townscape [Plate no. 4] invites comparison with village scenes by Sisley and Pissarro. As in several of his works, the horizon line for his perspective and some minor aspects of his composition approximate his stated interest in a 2:3 ratio [see p. 38]. Such correspondences are cumulative

[see p. 38]

FIGURE 18. Wilson Irvine, sketches of Ronda, Spain, 1929. From a sketchbook (Courtesy of Lydia Irvine Macdonald and Stewart Macdonald).

evidence of his adherence to this proportional formula as a rule-of-thumb device in laying out his compositions.

Irvine's sketchbooks are especially revealing for their record of this emphasis on composition. Although they contain a variety of isolated subjects (trees, rocks, horses, sheep, figures, vignettes from shipboard, boats, architecture, etc.) the most persistent feature is the landscape composition, often enframed as if it were already a prelude to painting [Fig. 18], and ranging from loosely stated ideas to more elaborate studies with color notations pencilled in and with dark and light patterns established. The variations among these compositional sketches are striking, indicative of his versatility in this genre. While his *plein air* painting may not have involved preparatory studies as normal procedure, he clearly exercised his sense of structure in his sketchbooks.

Occasionally, in Cornwall and elsewhere, Irvine photographed harbor and headlands, a form of documentation he may have used as references in his paintings. But it is clear from the journal entries that his normal *modus operandi* was to set up his easel on the spot and paint with an eye to the nuances of light and atmosphere that immediately confronted him [Fig. 19]. His journals of 1923 and 1929 are replete with observations on the weather and light — and upon these conditions depended the course of the day's work. If the sunshine changed to overcast he would take up another canvas, either a fresh one or one he had already begun under gray skies.

The Cornish coast, weather-fickle as it had proved to be, was yet stimulating to the artist. One Sunday at Zennor, after attending church and deploring the lackluster sermon, he went for a walk which he recorded in his journal: "What wonderful things these moors are. This afternoon I tramped over them to Gurnard's Head. Above you is a bold fence against the sky, stone and along it high gorse, a cloud shadow making them very dark against a distant sunlit hill strewn with gray rocks and covered with silvery green. Gates with great upright stones for posts. Then on to the head and a wonderful head it is. Its s[outh] slope is easy to the water and there are motifs simply great. A fine surf today. The view to the s[outh] great gashes in the rocks black against the sun, sparkling surf below, gulls soaring in the chasms. It's titanic cosmic unspoiled." Thus, on a Sunday evening back in the cottage he seemed to be painting in words the ephemeral pictures of the afternoon, as he struggled to keep a fire going in the "dam[ned] grates."[65]

Throughout the stay abroad Irvine read a great deal — daily newspapers, novels, histories, biographies — and commented regularly in his journal on his reading as well as on the political scene in Europe, for which he appeared to have a lively appetite. Evenings in St. Ives he and Lydia often attended the cinema whose fare was chiefly American, and on Sundays, not wishing to be dipped in the cold harbor, he frequently explored the countryside with his wife.

At Clovelly, some 80 miles or so up the coast from St. Ives, the Irvines spent only a week, the artist painting mostly on the grounds of Clovelly Court, a large estate. Leaving Clovelly, the Irvines arrived on June 10 at Betwys-y-Coed, a pleasant village about twelve miles east of Mount Snowden in northern Wales, where they quickly found a cottage with light housekeeping privileges. The following morning Irvine was out, scouting for subjects, and in the afternoon was at work on a painting in a nearby glen. As in Cornwall, the weather was unstable, but, typically, Irvine kept at his easel, changing canvases when the weather turned.

He was not at a loss for subjects. Betwys-y-Coed was one of the most famous mountain villages in Wales, much frequented by landscape artists, and for good reason. In its vicinity the Lledr and Conway valleys, rocky glens, falls where salmon and trout leaped upstream, picturesque stone bridges, some spanning deep gorges, upland meadows, and vistas of mountainous terrain dominated by the nearby heights of Moel Siabod, all provided Irvine with many choices.

A fine old stone bridge at Llanrwst [Cat. no. 27], a short distance north of Betwys-y-Coed, was a special treat for the artist. It was said to have been designed by Inigo Jones in the seventeenth century, but the attribution is doubtful.[66] On a misty gray morning with a sprinkling of rain in the air, he began to work. "Got down close to the pier and so had a foreshortened view

FIGURE 19. Wilson Irvine painting *en plein air* around Old Lyme.

of it and the great arch," he wrote. "It is most difficult to draw and drawing it causes one to bless the designer of it. The old cottage shows at the end, over the brook." The painting is solidly composed, emphasizing the thrust and rise of the bridge with its rhythm linked to the dormers on the cottage roof across the stream and the mass of the pier at the left joining the foreground to the distant hills. The bridge, the variegated gray stone work, the water, and the wooded landscape in the background, all respond to the cool, misty light under which he was working.

Irvine maintained his usual pace during some five weeks in Wales, commencing or finishing about fifteen canvases. He met other artists of varying degrees of competence, and a few of them sometimes painted with him, a practice he seems not to have welcomed but which he tolerated.

On July 28 the Irvines left Wales for Scotland via Lake Windermere, spending a night at Ambleside, and arrived in Glasgow the following day, having passed through Irvine, a place on Scotland's map which had fascinated the artist from his youth. They were in Glasgow only one night and left after a visit to the Glasgow Art Gallery and Museum, where Irvine was moved by Whistler's *Portrait of Thomas Carlyle: Arrangement in Gray and Black, No. 2.* "It has guts," he noted in his journal, "likewise all that is good in painting."

Two days later they were at Mallaig, on the west coast of Scotland, after a harrowing drive on poor narrow and twisting roads unprotected from sheer drops. Here they garaged the Ford and sailed for Stornoway on the Island of Lewis in the Outer Hebrides. The reason for going to this remote place was that John Bain, a Chicago banker, had commissioned Irvine to paint a portrait of his mother, who lived in Stornoway. The

island was not easy to reach. Their course was past the lower end of Skye, through the Sound of Sleat to Kyle, where they changed boats for the passage through the Inner Sound and into The Minch where the seas were rough. It was nearly midnight when they reached Stornoway and were greeted warmly by the Bain family.

Although the portrait of the elderly lady, some 84 years old and "keen" as she could be, was the artist's primary purpose on the island, he managed to paint some views of the town and harbor. *Harbor at Stornoway* [Cat. No. 28] is sensitively keyed throughout to the cold northern light, as if to register the chilliness of the air, and in establishing the perspective Irvine has set the horizon line in accord with his preference for a 2:3 ratio. There were also tours of Lewis and Harris islands with the Bains, a memorable visit to the Neolithic standing stones of Callanish, which fired Irvine's imagination as he envisioned ancient ceremonies among their haunting shapes,[67] a trip to a whaling station, the moors, the crofters' stone-and-sod cottages with thatched roofs, peat gatherers, and, back in Stornoway, the fishing boats with their sturdy masts. The weather ran a gray, wet, cold current through it all, for the sun's appearance was always brief and sporadic. By the time Irvine was to leave the island, both he and Lydia were longing for a warmer climate where the sun was not so seldom.

Irvine sold the Ford for twenty pounds, Scottish, to one of the islanders. It came over to Stornoway, in a storm, on the vessel he and Lydia were determined to take back to the mainland, foul weather notwithstanding. Since the car had cost Irvine twenty-three pounds, the sale was undoubtedly a good deal for the artist, although he complained that he would lose sixpence to the pound on it in England. Because of the storm, many who had booked passage earlier cancelled out, so the Irvines had no difficulty in getting berths on short notice — but they got little sleep. They sailed from Stornoway in the dark hours of the morning in the company of three hundred sheep, reached Mallaig shortly after noon, and boarded a train for Edinburgh, where a visit to the Scottish Academy exhibition convinced Irvine that it was "not nearly as good as our Academy show." He found the view from the ramparts of the castle quite lovely in the soft sunshine, but, in general, he did not fancy Edinburgh. It rained heavily that night and the next morning the Irvines were on their way by train to London and Dover, stayed one night in that coastal town, where Irvine was impressed by the soft moonlight on the pale chalk cliffs, sailed for Calais, and reached Paris that night.

Their first day in Paris was spent in walking along the Seine and visiting the Louvre and Luxembourg galleries. As was his custom, Irvine jotted down in his journal his reactions to some of the art he had seen during the day. He felt the "same as in 1908 about Rubens," and did not expand on the comment, but on the evidence of his remarks on later visits to European museums one can assume that his impressions were not entirely favorable. He "loved more" the likes of Raphael, Rembrandt, Leonardo da Vinci and especially "some of the old Italian masters, who for design & fine, gracious color could teach us a lot." He felt that the impressionist pictures in the Luxembourg were turning "muddy & dark," but Pissarro looked "better & better."[68]

At the American Express office on Monday, August 27, they waited anxiously for mail from home and were handed a cable telling them of the death of Irvine's sister, Ila, as well as the death of Lydia's brother. "What a ghastly wire," he wrote. A trip to Versailles that day did nothing to dispel their double grief.

Two days later they visited Les Andelys, then Giverny and the "wonderful" gardens of Claude Monet. Returning to Paris for one night, they boarded a train for Brittany on August 31. The previous day Irvine had written in his journal: "Glad to be on the way to Pont-Aven & what seemed like home because I had painted there in 1908."[69]

After a night at Quimperlé, which appeared in the early twilight more attractive to Irvine than he remembered it from 1908, they took an early morning train for Pont-Aven. Upon arrival Irvine walked about the town, noting that it had changed, but that it still looked good, although more prosperous due to the summer crowds. The following day, Sunday, he and Lydia walked around the neighborhood, enjoying the countryside, its orchards, tidy fields, and shadowy lanes, but, most of all, the sunshine.

They had secured lodgings and studio space at Ces Jours d'Or, formerly the Pension Gloanec, where Gauguin had resided in his prime Pont-Aven days.[70] In fact, the quarters Irvine and his wife occupied were said to be the same as Gauguin's, but this does not appear a deliberate choice on Irvine's part.

His initial efforts in Brittany seem somewhat nostalgic. On his first day of painting he began two canvases of subjects recalled from his earlier Breton experience: in the morning, the interior of the chapel at Trémalo, in the afternoon, Pont-Aven from a hill, and nearly the same view he had painted in 1908. But the sunny warmth of the first day gave way to gray on the second, and here, too, the weather proved somewhat unsteady. Gray day sometimes followed gray day, but, with warmer temperatures than in Great Britain and some fine sunny stretches along the way, Brittany was proving a good choice. On September 12, in nearby

FIGURE 20. Wilson Irvine, *Rooftops*, ca. 1923 [Cat. no. 30]. There is some question as to whether this view is in Brittany or Cornwall. (Private Collection)

Concarneau, he was working on a painting of boats with a part of the old city wall in the background — white and blue boats, red and yellow sails, blue masts, light spots of city beyond — and swore that he had wasted time at St. Ives. He wrote of this painting: "The first canvas I have done all through with yellow green, vermillion & blue purple and just spotting them in. I have an interesting start. My God but realism falls down when one sees the rot some of these chaps are doing…"

From time to time Irvine experienced — as he had at St. Ives — a stomach disorder which he usually blamed on the fish he ate. A French doctor prescribed a diet of eggs and boiled potatoes, which he tried to follow, but apparently had difficulty in making the help at the hotel understand that he wanted them served together.

However, his complaints were few and relatively minor during the two months at Pont-Aven. Typically, he was at his easel almost every day, often working on two canvases, one in the morning, the other in the afternoon, and with the enthusiasm generated by his finding so much in the Breton surroundings that he wanted to paint.

Even at night there was something to record. One weekend, as part of a Breton fête, a carousel was set up in the street right outside the Irvines' window. The effect of the lights and the crowd that gathered about so intrigued him that he painted the scene, a sparkling record of night festivities [Plate no. 9].

The chapel at Trémalo was a favored spot, as was the harbor at nearby Concarneau. The village streets [cf. Fig. 20], a couple of L'Aven river views, farm scenes, and the old mill at Pont-Aven in the moonlight were among the pieces he worked on during this period. He maintained the pace he had set throughout the trip, commencing or completing some twenty-two works in Brittany. It has often been said of Irvine that he was an extremely prolific painter. The record in his journals confirms this.

Before leaving Pont-Aven he reserved ship passage from Marseille on November 13 for Naples, Palermo, and home. On October 29 the Irvines left Pont-Aven by train for the south of France. Enroute, at Lyons, Irvine had time to visit the museum where he admired works by Puvis de Chavannes and Rodin, but did not like the early Corots. The next day they were on their way to Avignon where they found the streets thronged and the cafés full. They were tourists now. The next day was spent sightseeing, at Villeneuve-lès-Avignon across the Rhône where they enjoyed the view of Avignon from Fort Saint-André, then back to tour the Palace of the Popes and the gardens above the cathedral. The pace of their travels was quickening, as if to see as much as they could before boarding ship for the passage home. Between November 3, when they left Avignon, and November 13, when they sailed, they traveled to Marseille, Cannes, Nice, Monte Carlo, Grasse, Martigues (to which Irvine vowed to return someday to paint), Carcassonne, Montpellier, Nîmes, and back to Marseilles and their ship. There was no time for painting.

When their ship put in to Naples, they hired a

guide for a tour of the city, several churches, and the Museo Nazionale.[71] Here he liked the Titians and Ribera, found Correggio disappointing, and a Raphael "sweet as honey. Bah!" He praised a chest by Cellini, the antique marbles, bronzes from Pompeii, and a copy of the Prado *Los Borrachos* of Velasquez. The next day they visited Pompeii and Sorrento. On the following day they returned to the museum in the morning and in the late afternoon sailed for Palermo, arriving at sunrise. Here they visited the Cathedral, the Botanical Gardens, and the Museo Nazionale, where Irvine was attracted to the Greek vases and the Etruscan sarcophagi; but all of this must have been at a tourist's pace.

Sailing westward, the seas were rough but Irvine was back again playing chess and winning all his games, apparently able to keep the pieces on the board, unlike the Atlantic crossing months earlier. The ship skirted close enough to the African shore for the Atlas Mountains to be in view, and Irvine was surprised at their apparent height, but Gibraltar seemed to him much less impressive than the Prudential logo. In the Atlantic two days later, on November 23, the journal entries cease.

1924 to 1929

Upon returning to the United States Irvine must have been very busy preparing, for exhibition and sale, the work he had done abroad. In January he sent off to his friend and fellow Cliff Dweller, Chicago lawyer Percy B. Eckhart, who seems to have served as one of his dealers, eight of the recent canvases, three of which were immediately purchased by John Bain, who was deeply moved by Irvine's outright gift to him of the portrait of his mother which Irvine had painted at Stornoway. "You would have felt repaid for your efforts if you could have seen the genuine emotion which it caused him," wrote Eckhart. "He is more than pleased with it." As to the painting itself, Eckhart noted: "While I must admit that it isn't a Sargent in execution, it has got something that very few Sargents ever have in them — an insight into the character of the sitter and its very clear portrayal in the painting."[72]

In March of 1924 Irvine joined fellow Old Lyme painter Guy Wiggins in a showing of their work at Carper Galleries in Detroit, Michigan. Irvine may have been recalling the weather he had to cope with abroad when he remarked to a journalist covering the show that there was nothing that made more difference to a landscape painter than the kind of wind that was blowing.[73]

In April, Carson, Pirie, Scott and Company galleries in Chicago mounted a solo exhibition of twenty-six works by Irvine, consisting almost entirely of paintings from the trip abroad. A journalist from the *Chicago Herald Examiner*, in a perceptive review of the show, sensed a new quality in the artist's work. "Many painters, despite oncoming years, have remained youthful and questioning in their work… I think this is true of Irvine. I know that before I knew his age, and judging entirely from his paintings, I had formed the very definite opinion that he was one of the younger men. [Irvine was fifty-five when this was written.] His color was bright and happy, his manner of handling paint was spirited and, while informed, yet always gave me the impression of being the result of a constantly experimental attitude on the part of the painter." The reviewer continued, "Most of the new pictures were done abroad… It is beyond argument that each of these districts has a color and light all its own… Take

FIGURE 21. Wilson Irvine,
A Cottage in England, ca. 1923.
Present location unknown.

Irvine's paintings done about St. Ives in Cornwall. It is evident that he has had to deal with colors gauged and subdued and bound together into a tonality by a light perhaps filtered through Atlantic mists... Even in a canvas like '*The Fishing Fleet*' [now *St. Ives, Cornwall*, Plate No. 2], almost jewel-like in its color, there is a soberness and restraint that links it to the newer phase of Irvine's work. Although there has always been an engaging variety about Irvine's method of laying his pigments, I believe there is to be found in this European work evidence of a resolve to subdue his paint handling to conform to his more sober palette. Here and there, especially in the foreground of some of the landscape paintings, are to be found his old fireworks, but generally speaking, the paint is more methodically and carefully placed with a new care for drawing and values."[74]

A canvas of fishing boats beached by the ebb tide in the harbor at St. Ives [Plate no. 3] is a clearer instance than *St. Ives, Cornwall* of the new soberness the critic noted. The sunlight, barely breaking through the overcast, edges with silver the clouds over the uplands behind the town and the harbor basin, glistens brightly and coldly on the water beyond the boats, and highlights the flurry of gulls; but the general tone of the painting is darkening, as if the sunlight were transient and those "Atlantic mists" the constant agent in the Cornish weather. The boats in the foreground are somber silhouettes and town and uplands retire in purplish haze. It is a pictorial précis of Irvine's experience in the harbor town.

In August of 1924 a Boston reviewer of the Old Lyme summer show cited Irvine's recent work, *A Cottage in England* [Fig. 21], as "perhaps the finest painting in the exhibition, since it follows through to a pictorial balance... put together with a sure hand."[75] In mid-November he and Gregory Smith of Old Lyme were in a joint exhibition at the Rockford Art Association and in early December Irvine was in Grand Rapids, Michigan, attending to a showing at the Grand Rapids Art Gallery.[76] Also in December the *American Magazine of Art* proclaimed his *Morning at the Pool* one of the high spots of the Lyme Art Association exhibition. The same painting had also been honored by being selected as one of the illustrations in the catalogue of the National Academy of Design annual in 1923.

In May of 1925 Irvine was one of the painters who came to Atlanta, Georgia, in conjunction with an exhibition of works by artists associated with Grand Central Art Galleries in New York.[77] In November the Annex of the Wadsworth Atheneum in Hartford held a one-man exhibition of his work, a medley of New

England and European subjects, with one work, *Moose Cover, Quebec*, implying a recent visit to Canada. The catalogue cover reproduced *St. Ives, Cornwall*, then titled *The Fishing Fleet.* There were two works in the show of subjects from Martigues, which raises an interesting question. The journal of 1923 indicates that Irvine arrived at Martigues at noon on November 7 and left the next day for Carcassonne. There was no time for painting during the last three weeks in Europe, but Irvine did record that he took photographs at Martigues and was so impressed by the town, the canals, and the colorful boats that he promised himself, as noted earlier, to return some day to paint. If he made sketches, he did not say. However, in the spring of 1924 he had shown a Martigues subject at the National Academy of Design exhibition, possibly one of the works he later placed in the Hartford show, although the title varies slightly. It is evident, then, that these paintings were done, at least to some extent (and one quite completely), after photographs[78] and perhaps sketches — and memory — not in his customary way of working. But the fact that he also photographed in Great Britain earlier during the trip indicates that he was beginning to use photographs as documentary aids. To date, only one other painting done almost completely, and without question, after a photograph has come to light.[79] The evidence thus far does not argue for an extensive use of photographs by Irvine to establish entire compositions.

During the winter of 1925-26, at least from December into February, Irvine was busy in the wintry out-of-doors. On February 18 he wrote that he was "painting like a Trojan on the snow,"[80] which was going fast in a February thaw. It appears likely that *Heavy Snow* [Cat no. 35] was one of the works from these sessions, since both the warmth of the light and the obvious weight of the snow proclaim the thaw.

Also, about this same time, he may have been working on either his aquaprints or his prismatic paintings, more probably the latter: Lydia reported to their son Jan and his wife that "Dad has done *some very important things in a different way again* [italics added], he is feeling 10 years younger in ambition."[81]

On April 15, 1926, Irvine was elected an Associate Member of the National Academy of Design and fully confirmed at a meeting of the Council, December 22, when his mandatory self-portrait [Fig. 22] was accepted.[82] In May he was in Virginia to work on a painting of Westover, one of the great James River colonial mansions built by William Byrd around 1730.[83] Enroute he and Lydia had traveled through the Shenandoah Valley and into the Blue Ridge Mountains. In the early fall, when the autumn colors would have been at their peak, they visited Vermont.[84]

The following year *The Literary Digest* featured one of Irvine's finest snow scenes, *The Broken Wall* [Plate No. 21], on the cover of its February 5 issue. However, the reproduction of the painting was drastically cropped, right and left, to accommodate the magazine's format. In the spring he was represented by eight works in a large collection from Carson, Pirie, Scott which was exhibited in Joliet, Illinois. Irvine was in interesting company: also in the exhibition were works by George Bellows, Winslow Homer, Henry Ward Ranger, Willard Metcalf, Bruce Crane, Victor Higgins, Frederick Frieseke, and Guy Wiggins, among numerous others, well-known and otherwise.[85]

Although Irvine had been creating monotypes (or monoprints) at least as early as 1913,[86] around 1927 he began to produce some unique variations on the medium in a series of "aquaprints" [see Cat. Nos. 36, 37]

FIGURE 22. Wilson Irvine, *Self-Portrait*, 1926 (National Academy of Design).

which were exhibited that summer at the Lyme Art Association, in the early fall at Milch Galleries in New York, from mid-October to early November at Curtis H. Moyer galleries in Hartford, and from November 15 to November 30 at Albert Roullier Galleries in Chicago. These prints were modifications of the old Japanese method of making the marbleized paper later used so extensively in Europe and America as end papers in the binding of fine books. Irvine's process seems to have involved laying down the colors on a liquid surface (possibly a water-gum solution in a shallow pan) in such a way as to suggest landscape or figural motifs and then floating the paper on this surface to pick up the patterns of color. Following this, some additional accents or painted areas would transform the work into a more specific image. These prints tended to be much more abstract in character than his usual work. Their production appears to have been limited to a relatively brief period around 1927. Irvine also produced etchings, but this medium did not engage him on a level comparable to his painting.

During the winter of 1927-28 Irvine was in New Orleans. He informed a journalist that the reason he had come there was that twenty-five years ago he had a passion for reading George W. Cable and never forgot. He "had a mild word of praise for the renovated courts of the quarter," the reporter noted, "but kept his unstinted encomium for the old grey places where the walls are decaying. Almost shyly, he told of a great old neglected courtyard [Cat. no. 38] where he found an old man selling birds [Plate no. 10]. He said the old fellow moved his wagons and the horses he stables, in order to give the artist room…"[87] At one point Irvine apparently told the journalist that he intended to return to New Orleans every winter. The next winter, however, he was in Europe.

To france and spain

The Irvines sailed from New York on December 21, 1928, and arrived at Boulogne-sur-Mer on January 1. Before noon on the day of arrival they reached Paris. The next morning Irvine shopped for painting materials and in the cold afternoon toured the city, visiting the Palais de Justice and admiring the stained glass windows of Sainte-Chapelle. On January 3 they were on their way by train to Marseille amid heavy snow and in the afternoon of January 5 were in Martigues, fulfilling Irvine's promise to himself in 1923 that he would come back to paint. He walked about, finding some changes, especially a red iron bridge. "Progress raises hell with lady beauty," he noted. The next day, Sunday, he spent wandering the streets and the edges of town and on Monday began to paint. He was pleased thus far: "It's stuff that's different from our mild hues & hillsides & has to be learned. Boy! When that fisherman raised his red lateen sail over a green & blue boat against those pale yellow buildings, all reflected in the quiet water, I could have shouted."

By mid-January things changed — the mistral began to blow, fierce and cold, even on sunny days. He would finish a day of painting tired out from fighting the wind. "It's hell to wake up in the morning after having endured three days of this miserable mistral wind & see the cedars in a neighbor's yard threshing about and know you have to endure another day of it. Clear light, not a cloud but a wind impossible to work in." (One recalls how Vincent van Gogh had struggled with the mistral when he was in Arles.) And it was cold: "Colder than standing in snow at 10 above in Conn[ecticut]." Sometimes, under these conditions, he walked about, taking photographs.

About a week before leaving for Spain he had perfect weather for painting and Martigues was a delight. At the end of January he had one of the best days so far: "Started a thing of some white houses done through the prism. The first go at it made my other things look gray & lifeless." The matter-of-fact phrasing implies that this practice of utilizing the prism's refracted light in viewing a subject was not a breakthrough at Martigues, but something he had done before. This gives some credence to Lydia's letter of 1926 [see p. 33], citing Irvine's new way of working "again", as being a reference to his experiments in prismatic painting.

As if the mistral had not been enough of an annoyance, Irvine was tormented throughout his stay at Martigues by the attentions of an amateur French painter who insisted on hanging around while the American was at work, sometimes taking notes. "I have given him $200 in lessons, by his standing over me," Irvine remarked. Still, it had been a productive month — fifteen works were begun or completed. Upon leaving Martigues some were packed wet and he feared for those done with the palette knife.

After one full day in Marseille they were on their way to Spain. Always on the *qui vive* for likely places to paint, Irvine found little en route to interest him. From Madrid, where they stayed overnight and which seemed "lovely in the early morning haze", they went sharply south for Ronda. It was dark when they reached there on February 12 and Ronda did not at first look interesting, but a short walk that night gave promise.

After acquainting himself with the town and its immediate surroundings Irvine was soon at work, fascinated by a stone bridge over the deep gorge [see Fig. 18, page 26], the strings of burdened donkeys trudging up from the mills below, the old bull ring, and the courtyards and cobblestone streets. But there were drawbacks, too: sometimes it was cold, wet, and windy; there were numerous beggars, very young to very old; and the local youngsters were a constant source of harrassment, hovering about as he painted, hollering, whistling, rolling stones towards him. When he complained at the hotel and suggested that he might be forced to leave, the hotel owner went to the chief of police and the mayor, who assigned a policeman to keep the enemy at bay. When painting in the courtyards he was sometimes badgered by the people living there, but by paying for the privilege of setting up his easel — which he felt was only fair — he was able to lessen the tension and get on with his work.

While in Ronda Irvine met two brothers, one of whom was an artist and follower of Picasso, who was born not far away, in Malaga. Irvine met the two young Spaniards on several occasions and there were discussions of Picasso's art — judging from the journal entries, his cubism in particular. The young Spanish artist said he liked Irvine's work. "But I know that is a Spanish way of being polite," Irvine wrote in his journal, "for what radical painter can see virtue not done according to the Cézanne or Picasso formula — none." His reaction to the young Spaniard seems to have been somewhat ambivalent: he stated that he was charming and a good painter, yet Irvine's description of his work seems far from being an endorsement. "Curious scratches he called two nudes. Work out to a finish the gold braid on a toreador's costume & do the head & hands modernistically!" Possibly this was merely a description, but it smacks somewhat of criticism however restrained by his respect for the young man. In New Orleans the previous winter Irvine was reported to have said that the "new" art (no explanation as to

FIGURE 24. Wilson Irvine, *Grazalema Range, Spain*, 1929 (Private Collection), and a pencil sketch of the range, 1929, from one of his sketchbooks. (Courtesy of Lydia Irvine Macdonald and Stewart Macdonald)

Lydia were anxiously awaiting news from their eldest son, Ted, who had recently married and was traveling in Europe with his wife. They were planning to join Irvine and his wife in Ronda. They arrived on March 13 to find Irvine ready to be off to the north. The next day they all went on a day trip to Grazalema, a hill town a few miles west of Ronda. Irvine was impressed by the cloud-shadowed mountains, gray, bare, rocky, that overlooked the town in which every alley seemed to end in a gray peak. They had tea at a small inn where the artist Ernest Martin Hennings, whom Irvine must have known from the Chicago years, had stayed for two months and found his "charming" entry in a guest book.[89] A pencil sketch and a painting, *The Grazalema Range, Spain* [Fig. 24], the latter exhibited later in 1929, commemorate the brief visit. The painting, however, could not have been done in Spain [see p. 43].

Leaving Ronda, all four went on to Grenada, visiting the Alhambra — lovelier than Irvine had realized. In Madrid Irvine's visit to the Prado was an intense experience. "Goya!... How one lingers over Goya's things." Irvine came back to the Prado the following day and spent most of his time with the Goyas. But it was the Velasquez *Las Meninas* that he pronounced the finest painting he had ever seen — "space was never better expressed." He was not as keen about that painter's *Surrender of Breda* or his *Triumph of Bacchus* (or *Los Borrachos*, the copy of which had so intrigued him in Naples in 1923). He admired El Greco's color — "one can understand his vogue" — and he seemed surprised that he liked Veronese, but Tiepolo's color was disappointing. He felt that he was constantly running into sources of movements in art and proclaimed the visit to the Prado the "greatest day entertainment" of his life.

It was arranged the following day that Irvine's

precisely what he meant by that) had done one fine thing, if nothing else, by liberating "thousands of people from the fear that they could not paint because they could not draw" and that this would "at least stimulate a wider interest in art."[88] Apparently, at Ronda, he was not yet of a mind to extend his approbation of modernity much beyond his 1923 approval of Gauguin.

By early March Irvine was getting restive. He and

party could tour the palace of the Duke of Alba, who happened to be away at that time. This was another fine experience for Irvine — "3 hours of delight." He found the tapestries of East Indian subjects the finest he had ever seen and, again, Goya and El Greco were among the high points.

At the Escorial his enthusiasm focused on a Cellini crucifix, a "good Ribera & a wonderful El Greco" which made one realize "what a master El Greco was." But he felt that the tapestries designed by Goya were not up to the cartoons for them which he had seen in the Prado.

A day trip to Toledo resulted in first impressions that were disappointing, for the the hill was not as high as Irvine anticipated and the bridges were not up to his expectations. There were, however, compensations. He found things that reminded him of Cervantes, and in S.Tomé he saw El Greco's *Burial of Count Orgaz*, "a supreme piece of decoration." The house of El Greco was "holy ground", the studio "a shrine", and the Museo El Greco contained a series of El Greco Apostles and a fine portrait by Velasquez. Nevertheless, he found Toledo itself somewhat less than he had expected.

Segovia, on the other hand, Irvine loved at first sight. Rising from a hilltop, it was somewhat like Toledo, but "very much more interesting" to the artist. There were fine churches and monasteries, the immense cathedral, the aqueduct, pale yellow-toned houses that glowed in the moonlight, and winding streets with motifs at every turn. There were "fine gardens in the valley, pollard willows, fresh green, spring buds & blossoms everywhere. Never saw so many things to do in so small a space." Even the children seemed better than in Ronda — but, after all, they were untested for he was not setting up his easel here.

Irvine found subjects galore, remarking that Segovia got better each time he stirred out. On a walk in the valley below Segovia with Ted, he made some pencil sketches and vowed to return in 1931. To date, there is no evidence that he did.

Before leaving by train for Santander on the Bay of Biscay, Irvine, early in the morning, walked about Segovia one last time, savoring its ambiance. At Hendaye, on the French border, the elder Irvines parted from Ted and his wife and arrived at Paris late that evening.

The next two days Irvine spent in the Louvre, viewing "miles of great things & and tens of miles of old hats." Some of his old idols had "crumbled" and "new gods" had risen. His journal gives us hints. Veronese, whose work had surprised him at the Prado, was still better, and he was especially enthusiastic over Leonardo da Vinci.[90] He liked Ribera and Watteau (an interesting combination) and he "drank in the Dutch who didn't have to paint by the square rod to impress." He praised Courbet as "one of the greatest of masters" (possibly one of his "new gods") and enjoyed the Greek vases and the Japanese art. And somehow, he felt, the Primitives (the early Italian painters he had admired so much in 1923) seemed the best of all.

But Rembrandt did not appeal as strongly as in the past, and there were others. "Certainly the Barbizon school all of them have slipped a cog and I am on shaking ground. Same with most of the impressionists. Few have kept their lustre or interest in surface quality or design. Design seems more important."[91] The self-doubts raised in his reassessment of impressionism and its Barbizon predecessors may have been a spur to his prismatic experiments, but the comment on design was quite another matter.

Design had always been a important aspect of

Irvine's painting, even to the extent that he sometimes applied a proportional scheme to his compositions. In one of his sketchbooks that may date to around 1908 there is a notation stressing the importance of the "rule of 2 to 3", which he sketchily diagrammed in a half-dozen different examples having the hasty look of lecture notes [Fig. 25]. An analysis of several of his paintings reveals this 2:3 formula at work, at least as a rule-of-thumb [Fig. 26]. In this respect, Irvine parallels a number of other artists of his time, like George Bellows, for instance, whose interest in Jay Hambidge's "dynamic symmetry" and the "golden section" has been well documented.[92]

FIGURE 25. Wilson Irvine, notes on 2:3 proportion from one of his sketchbooks. (Courtesy of Lydia Irvine Macdonald and Stewart Macdonald)
His notation, in eccentric abbreviated form, translates as "Rule of 2 to 3 through all nature. In leaves, in beings—in all bones and muscles of the body" and "In square must be at points or point (point of interest)."

FIGURE 26. Diagrams of works by Irvine, demonstrating his extensive use of the 2:3 proportional system as a "rule of thumb" in composing his paintings.

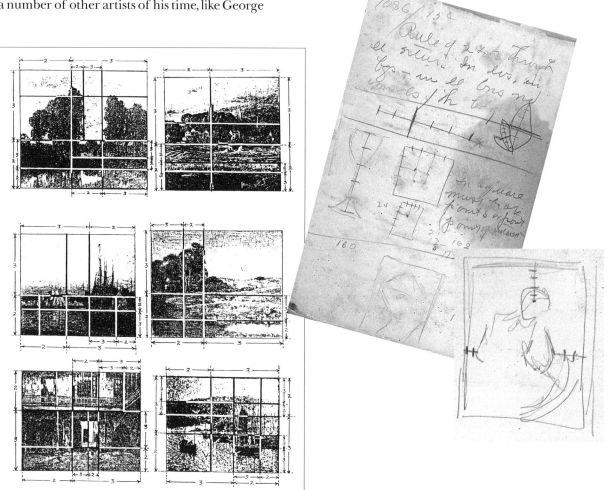

THE LAST YEARS

The Irvines arrived back in the United States around the middle of April, 1929, having sailed from Cherbourg on April 3. There is no account of the return voyage, since Irvine's journal ends in Paris on April 1. For the remainder of that year, during which he was awarded the Noel Flagg Prize in the exhibition of the Connecticut Academy of Fine Arts, he must have been preoccupied with developing his prismatic paintings since in March of 1930 he showed twenty-two of them at Grand Central Art Galleries in New York. Some had already been shown in the 1929 summer exhibition at Old Lyme, eliciting from *The New York Times*' conservative art critic, Edward Alden Jewell, some smugly sarcastic observations: "Wilson Irvine has come back, from wherever it is he has been, tipsy with prism madness. Nearly all his pictures are prismatic in their coloring. You see a 'Studio Window' bathing the objects behind which it is placed in a startling iridescence, and you think, well, possibly the window was stained glass. But then you see a landscape without any window at all, and the same effect is sovereign. So then you know that Mr. Irvine is passing through a 'phase'."[93] The reviewer from *The Christian Science Monitor* saw it differently and wrote that Irvine's works, including *The Studio Window*, "argue a fine pictorial talent, sure and brilliant, replete with strong drawing, and rich in color."[94] *The Boston Post* had praise at some length for Irvine's *The Grazalema Range, Spain* and noted "a still life in glowing prismatic color."[95]

Precisely when Irvine began to experiment with viewing his subjects through a prism is not known, perhaps as early as 1926, or even earlier.[96] In his statement for the catalogue of the 1930 exhibition at Grand Central Art Galleries he explained this new direction in his work. Any object viewed through a prism, he stated, developed around its edges a halo of refracted light, more greenish against a light background and more reddish against a dark, and he began to paint these prismatic effects. He pointed out that when the prism was held horizontally there was little prismatic effect on the perpendicular edges, but when the prism was held in a slanted position there was color dispersion along the perpendiculars. [*The author has experimented with viewing through a prism a variety of objects under varying conditions of lighting and, although the green or red dominance can be observed, and tilting the prism does change the location of halos, the pattern seems more complicated than Irvine's explanation.*][97] Irvine utilized this technique in still lifes, landscapes, and figural paintings. When it was applied with subtlety the effect is quietly luminous without being intrusive [see Cat. Nos. 40, 43, 44, 45, Plates No. 12, 13, 14]. When more boldly rendered, these optical effects could be somewhat startling in the context of an otherwise impressionistic painting, not unlike color printing when slightly off-register. And when the prismatic contours are thus so strongly assertive the effect is to edge his palette towards an optically agitated, slightly acidic tonality. Irvine had hoped that his prismatic experiments and the principles they involved "would really mean something to painters," but the initial flurry of interest which greeted these works was neither enthusiastic nor sustained, although he himself continued to produce prismatic paintings during the remainder of his career. His idea received some national exposure when *A Prismatic Winter Landscape* was featured on the cover of the January 31, 1931 issue of *The Literary Digest*.

In his prismatic mode Irvine may have turned a sharper corner than he realized — or was prepared to pursue. It remained, for that reason, in a limbo of untapped possibilities for himself as well as for other artists, but it is not unreasonable to suggest that in its understated way it was a quiet and forgotten adumbration of later optical art. The fact that his innovation was tethered to an impressionist point-of-view, however much it stretched the connection, assured its being soon overlooked by others.

By this time impressionism had long since relinquished its place at the leading edge of western painting. Successive waves of European modernism had altered the art scene so extensively that Irvine was caught in the eddy of what was increasingly viewed as an outmoded style. Although it would be some time before modernism assumed anything like a truly dominant role in American art, the American art scene had shifted considerably since Irvine's Chicago years and the Old Lyme colony's heyday. By the time Irvine began to gain recognition beyond a regional level in the Midwest — let us say between 1908 and 1912 — the international art scene was already feeling the full impact of European modernism, soon to buffet the New York art world in the Armory Show of 1913. Alfred Stieglitz, for example, had opened his gallery at 291 Fifth Avenue in 1905 and in 1908 held a Matisse exhibition, that artist's first solo show outside of Paris. The following year the gallery featured, among others, exhibitions of John Marin, Alfred Maurer, and Marsden Hartley. Between 1911 and 1913 there were solo exhibitions at 291 of such European masters as Cézanne, Matisse, and Picasso in addition to American modernists like Max Weber, Hartley, and Arthur Dove. However, there was still a private market for impressionist works and Irvine was able to live comfortably through the sales of his paintings.

In 1924 Irvine was reported to have said, "Any painter who in this day and age clings tenaciously to the one thing which he can do best, in a technical sense, and is satisfied, is not only standing still; he is actually retrograding."[98] With reference to his 1923 trip to Great Britain and France, he was said to remark, "I determined to get new impressions and to start afresh in all things when I went abroad. I left my palette, brushes and paints at home. In London I bought new square brushes. Before that I used round brushes. I found a different palette and chose a new make of colors and a new easel. Everything was different."[99] But, after all, these were only the materials of the painting craft.

Despite his avowal of the felicities of change — and his experimentation beyond the normal perimeters of impressionism — he remained essentially an impressionist painter, partial and sensitive to the attractions of the natural world and responsive to the transient light and atmosphere in each experience of it. Being inherently a *plein air* painter, Irvine to some degree surrendered himself to his subject, an act of sublimation in which the process of recreating the visual identity of the scene immediately before him partially absorbed his own. This humble response to the innate features and transitory conditions of his landscape subjects appears generally to have transcended any stylistic self-consciousness. One is usually first aware of the subject — its mood, light, and atmosphere — when viewing one of Irvine's paintings. The rest comes later.

His remark about liking to paint when there was "a kind of hazy beauty in the air" is seldom better illustrated than in *Cool Shadows* [Plate no. 11]. Here the sentient recording of light and atmosphere seems even to evoke some hint of summer sultriness, as if the artist were totally absorbed into the conditions of the moment in this particular place. While the brushwork registers tactile qualities as distinct from one another as the mirror of the pond and the foliage of the trees, it also develops a unifying surface texture for the painting as a whole. The lushness and air of summer lassitude are in sharp contrast to another painting of somewhat similar composition, *Stream Drift* [Plate no. 8].

In this typically impressionistic canvas the mood is late autumnal. The sense of light and the substance of things appear so intermingled in the microstructure of broken color that they merge their separate identities into a common element almost as wispy as a cloud. The blue sky, faintly infused with a warm undertone, barely draws the scene away from the edge of melancholy. If that subjective mood would appear to be best served by vaporous or ambiguous images, another of Irvine's landscapes contradicts the assumption.

Stone Wall at Old Lyme [Plate no. 20] is both more specifically descriptive and more truly melancholy. The sullen sky is the key to the painting's general tone, pensive, elegiac. The downward slope of the land as it recedes towards distant hills, the pointed boulder in the foreground, the faint wheel tracks, the converging stone walls, the screen of leafless trees feathered against the sky, all conspire to lead the viewer to the white farmhouse in the middle distance. The reciprocal sentiments of loneliness and refuge dominate the picture's mood.

A review in the *New York Tribune* of the 1922 annual Lyme Art Association exhibition, in citing the entries of Wilson Irvine and Guy Wiggins, noted: "Nothing that either of these men shows hints of the studio. We feel that they have painted with their easels planted outdoors, and that at times they have had to fight mos-

FIGURE 27. Irvine painting in his studio at his Hamburg residence. His daughter-in-law, Josephine, is posing. Photograph by Peter Juley.

quitoes or to blow on their fingers to keep them warm."[100] The freshness and immediacy of *The Broken Wall* [Plate no. 21] would appear to support the critic's surmise. It is a quintessential winter landscape and one of Irvine's most effective and complex compositions.[101] If the artist re-orchestrated the scene before him for purely compositional purposes, he did not lose touch with its reality. Both the snow-covered foreground slope, in chilly shadow mottled by patches of light filtered through the evergreens, and the sunlit snowfield beyond the wall convey perfectly the appropriate winter tones. The irregular line of the stone wall and the delicate parallelogram implied by the opening between the trees and its framing trunks and

FIGURE 28. The Old Lyme artists with Mr. and Mrs. William O. Goodman of Chicago in 1928. Irvine is fourth from the right and Florence Griswold third from the left. The Goodmans established an annual prize award for the Lyme Art Association and in 1934 it was won by Wilson Irvine.

FIGURE 29. Wilson Irvine, *Indolence*, ca. 1934. Present location unknown.

branches define a diagonal thrust in the composition. While this is reinforced by the bases of the foremost trees and by a suggestion of a triangular wedge from the foremost tree at the right through the opening in the wall, the cadences formed by the tree trunks on the slope in front stabilize the underlying linear structure of the composition and imply a near-symmetry that almost makes a triptych of the painting.

During the final years of his life Irvine seems to have spent more time than formerly in the studio with figure painting and still life [Fig. 27], and with exploring his prismatic mode. Around 1932, however, he must have visited Charleston, South Carolina, for the summer exhibition at the Lyme Art Association that year included some work indicating, as one reviewer put it, that he had "discovered Charleston as containing some of the few remaining traces of antiquity which America has preserved" and had made a "pat-

tern of brilliant harmony out of the crumbling plastered walls" and the transparent shadows that graced them.[102]

In 1934 Irvine was awarded the Mr. and Mrs. William O. Goodman Prize at the Lyme Art Association exhibition [Fig. 28], for a reclining nude, *Indolence* [Fig. 29], which drew from Edward Alden Jewell another review, treating with thinly-veiled scorn the prismatic mode in which the prize-winning work and others were painted. With reference to the prize, Jewell remarked, "Summer after Summer Mr. Irvine has been exhibiting at Old Lyme, pictures whose forms are outlined in rainbow... and the other day persistence in the pursuit of a theory was rewarded... Need one have recourse to arbitrary procedures such as this in order positively to prevent one's pictures being mistaken for pictures by anyone else? Fortunately, no."[103] The critic's shot was way off the mark.

Evidence from Irvine's art throughout his career,

and from his journals as well, refutes Jewell's presumptuous speculations as to the artist's intentions. Irvine's thrust as a painter was never towards discovering a device to stamp his work as distinct from that of other artists. Rather, his focus was on the situation at hand. His efforts aimed consistently and honestly at the means with which to record the uniqueness of each subject in a world where transience is the rule. His prismatic paintings were intense explorations of the nature of light. As such, they reached for a sheen of light which would evoke, with radically enhanced intensity, the actual sensation of vibrancy in the original sensory experience by exploring a prismatic reality which lay hidden within the natural luminosities that had always challenged him as he sought their valid equivalents on the canvas [Fig. 30]. This is clearly the case with *The Marshes* [Plate no. 12], in which the wetlands in the foreground and the distant landscape emit a somber glow suggestive of the light that lingers as the daylight fades, a quality reinforced by the prismatic notes. And in both *Cal, the Widower* [Cat. no. 40] and *Lady in Red* [Plate no. 13] the interior light is subtly enhanced by the prismatic elements.

His aquaprints seem, by comparison, to have been temporary experiments in a transfer technique, fascinating and inventive, but essentially a creative aside for one who was essentially a *painter*. The fact that they remain a mode apart from the general continuity of his art suggests that their fundamental nature, so much a hostage to chance, ran somewhat against the artist's grain once he had satisfied his curiosity as to their properties. They did not lead him, as they might have, to new directions in his painting.

There are also other veins in his art that run contrary to the normal pattern, evidence of his range but essentially isolated examples. At times an expressionis-

tic vigor, kinesthetic in nature, flares up in his execution, signaling the sheer exhilaration of the painting act itself. Surely this was the "fireworks" to which the Chicago critic alluded in the review of Irvine's show at the Carson, Pirie, Scott galleries in 1924.

Yet another example strikes an entirely different note: chromatically austere, *The Grazalema Range, Spain* [Fig. 24], emphasizes the rugged leanness of an arid, rocky landscape boldly rendered in a busy pattern of twisting rhythms and jostling planes. Although great distances are implied, the actual visual effect is of space compressed. It could not have been painted on the spot since Irvine was there for only part of a day and no mention is made in the artist's journal of painting on that brief visit; but in one of his sketchbooks containing Spanish subjects from that trip there is a pencil sketch that depicts the Grazalema range. Since the painting could not have been done there, but in Connecticut upon his return, Irvine had to rely on memory and the sketch, or, perhaps, a photograph as well. This may account for the singularity of the work, which, in its simplified and rather flattened landscape forms, is somewhat post-impressionistic in feeling.

During his last year Irvine was in poor health and on August 21, 1936 he died of a cerebral hemorrhage in his home at Hamburg. Upon learning of his death, Peter van Valkenburgh, a portrait painter and boyhood friend, wrote to the artist's widow from his home in California of his great respect for that "buoyant and gallant personality" who had been denied the fruitful years of his seasoned maturity.[104] Years later, on the occasion of an exhibition of works by artists associated with the Old Lyme colony held at Grand Central Art Galleries, the director recalled "the sensitive and dignified Wilson Irvine."[105] Irvine projected a unique blend of professional integrity and personal charm, well documented through his art, his journals, correspondence, and the memories of others. As his old friend noted, he was buoyant, with that elasticity of spirit that often accompanies an enthusiasm for fresh experiences of people and places when it is joined to a sense of humor with which to temper them. Although dedicated to his craft, he was not so totally immersed in his own persona as to be careless or unmindful of others, for he devoted considerable energy to the professional organizations to which he belonged and to social relationships involving his friends and his family. His affection for his wife — and their interdependence — surfaces again and again in the journals. His

daughter, Lois, recalled that "his modesty and charm of manner endeared him to countless friends."

Finally, some phrases garnered from William Wordsworth's *Lines Composed a Few Miles Above Tintern Abbey…* seem appropriate to the spirit of Wilson Irvine's engagement with the natural world he so often painted, for nature then to him "was all in all… an appetite; a feeling and a love, that had no need of a remoter charm." And if poetry is, as some would say, a transcendent distillation of experience, then one might add that the most pervasive and enduring element in Irvine's art would very likely be his regard for the poetic, transforming power of nature's light.

FIGURE 30. Wilson Irvine painting *Lois and Betty-June,* ca. 1932, shown in the Winter Exhibition at the National Academy of Design, November-December, 1932. The painting is in the prismatic mode. It was selected as one of the exhibition's catalogue illustrations.

NOTES

1. Statement attributed to Irvine in Florence Davis, "The Artists' Velvet Tie Gives Way to Hip Boots," *Detroit News*, March 16, 1924. Archives of American Art, Microfilm Reel 1233, Frame 160.

2. Jeffrey W. Andersen, "The Art Colony at Old Lyme," *Connecticut and American Impressionism* (Exh. cat., Storrs, Connecticut: The William Benton Museum of Art, The University of Connecticut, 1980) 114-149. On "tonalism" see Wanda M. Corn, *The Color of Mood: American Tonalism 1880-1910* (Exh. cat., San Francisco: M.H.DeYoung Memorial Museum and the California Palace of the Legion of Honor, 1972).

3. *Bulletin of The Art Institute of Chicago*, X, 8 (December, 1916) 234. Correspondence in the Irvine Archives at the Florence Griswold Museum indicates that the artist and Mrs. Irvine were in Hamburg during the summer of 1917, but returned to Chicago in October.

4. In 1980 William H. Gerdts curated a major exhibition and wrote its important catalogue essay, *American Impressionism* (Seattle: The Henry Art Gallery, The University of Washington, 1980). That same year a unique exhibition featuring three simultaneous venues was held in Connecticut: *Connecticut and American Impressionism*, curated by Jeffrey W. Andersen, Susan G. Larkin, and Harold Spencer with general oversight of the three exhibitions provided by Hildegard Cummings, Curator of Education, The William Benton Museum of Art. Numerous exhibitions with regional emphasis followed. During the 1980s there were two exhibitions of Wilson Irvine's work in Chicago: *Wilson Irvine*, at Mongerson Gallery in June of 1983 and *Wilson Henry Irvine, A.N.A. (1869-1936)* at Campanile Galleries that fall. In 1990 there were two exhibitions: *The Art of Wilson Irvine*, at Adams Davidson Galleries, Washington, D.C., which went on to The Bruce Museum, Greenwich, Connecticut, and *Wilson Henry Irvine, Old Lyme Impressionist* at the Connecticut Gallery, Marlborough, Connecticut.

5. For a fuller account of these matters, see Harold Spencer, "Reflections on Impressionism, Its Genesis and American Phase," *Connecticut and American Impressionism*, pp. 42-46, 51.

6. Newton Bateman, Paul Selby, Horace G. Kauffman, and Rebecca H. Kauffman, editors, *Historical Encyclopedia of Illinois and History of Ogle County* (Chicago: Munsell Publishing Co., 1909) 645, 751-752, 819. *Bicentennial History of Ogle County* (Ogle County Board, Ogle County, Illinois, 1976) 224, 411. The History of Ogle County, Illinois (Chicago: H.F.Kett & Co., 1878) 592, 594-595. *Portrait and Biographical Record of Winnebago and Boone Counties, Illinois* (Chicago: Biographical Publishing Co., 1892) 424-426.

7. *Historical Encyclopedia of Illinois and History of Ogle County*, p. 647. Edwin A. Irvine's obituary, *The Rockford Morning Star*, December 2, 1911, reported that he served with the 92nd Illinois Infantry and was a member of a military guard that saw the safe transportation of some $20,000,000 sent from San Francisco to the subtreasury in New York in 1862. He was a charter member of the Cooling Post, Grand Army of the Republic, No. 316, Byron, Illinois, which was chartered July 25, 1883.

8. *Historical Encyclopedia of Illinois...*, p. 688. *Rockford City Directory*. 1887-88, p. 218. This was the Chicago, Milwaukee & St. Paul Railroad, which had built a line from Chicago into Ogle County as far as Byron by 1875, and beyond the county by 1880.

9. Ila Irvine studied drama in New York and appeared on the stage prior to her marriage in 1896 to John M. Emmott, who died in 1911. Ila served as director of physical culture for the Rockford School System from about 1903 until 1910, and from about 1907 until 1916 as instructor in elocution at Rockford College. She directed several plays, performed monologues, and toured professionally as an elocutionist. After World War I she served in Washington, D.C., chairing the Women's National Republican Congressional Committee. The author is indebted to Mr. John Molyneaux, Local History and Genealogy, Rockford Public Library, Rockford, Illinois, for the above information. Sources: Rockford city directories; Rockford College yearbooks; Obituary, Ila Irvine Emmott, *The Rockford Morning Star*, August 22, 1923; Obituary, John M. Emmott, *The Rockford Morning Star*, November 19, 1911. Information on Irvine's accompanying his sister to school and on their mother's ambitions for her children is from a typescript, apparently of an unidentifed newspaper article (ca. 1924), in the Irvine files of the Rockford Art Museum.

10. *The National Cyclopedia of American Biography*, XLII (New York: James T. White & Co., 1958) 358-359. The entry was probably supplied largely by the family. No firm documentation of Irvine's newspaper employment has yet to come to light. The artist's granddaughter, Lydia Irvine Macdonald, informs the author that Irvine also did commercial work for Sears Roebuck during the early Chicago years, and produced a series of paintings for a prominent theater chain to install in its lobbies.

11. *Catalogue: Rockford High Schools 1862-1914* (Rockford, Illinois, 1914) 28. *Rockford High School Annual* (1912) 74: "Wilson H. Irvine, '88, has perhaps brought the class the highest fame. His name is recognized among those who are bringing credit to the City of Chicago." Irvine is also reported to have attended Jennings Seminary in Aurora, Illinois, around 1888, but this has yet to be confirmed, since the institution — then a fine private high school — ceased operations in 1942 and the matriculation records have not been located. Informants in the area indicate that these records may not have been preserved. Vernon Derry, "Aurora's First High School," *Thrift Corner Yarns*, Vol. 98 (Aurora, Illinois, September 1970), courtesy Aurora University Library. Correspondence with Archives, Northern

Illinois Conference, United Methodist Church, Evanston, Illinois, and Aurora Historical Society.

12. Wilson Irvine, *Diary*, 1888, under entries for March 1-3.

13. Information from artist's grandson, Joseph P. Irvine. Private Archives.

14. The author is indebted to John L. Molyneaux for this information. Correspondence dated August 14, 1996. References: Rockford city directories; see also *Description and Price of the Air Brush* (Rockford, Illinois: Air Brush Manufacturing Co., Gazette Printing House, 1887). The Illinois Art School does not appear in the *Rockford City Directory* after 1902, so it was probably discontinued around that time. Mr. Andy Penaluna, of Swansea, Wales, U.K., is currently working on a history of the airbrush. He has kindly supplied the author with information on the early Rockford model, which apparently was a difficult instrument to master until later improvements were made.

15. See end of footnote 9. In this typescript Irvine is reported to have worked in the "Air Brush Studio" in Rockford after graduation from high school. Although his 1888 diary confirms his use of the airbrush, it makes no reference to this studio — or to any employment. If Irvine returned to Rockford temporarily following his business school studies in Chicago, no evidence of it has come to light. The three years between his departure from Rockford and his marriage to Lydia Weyher in 1891 were certainly an important period for Irvine, but no record of it has yet been found.

16. Undated and unidentified newspaper clipping. Private Archives. From internal evidence it is clear that it was a Rockford newspaper and that it was from the issue of April 9, 1891. Mr. John Molyneaux informs me that the clipping may be from the *Rockford Republican*, later the *Rockford Republic*, but no files of this newspaper have been located prior to 1896. Since this item does not appear in other Rockford newspapers at that time, the above newspaper is, by default, the likely source.

17. It is possible that Wilson Irvine was encouraged to pursue a career in art by the example of one of his uncles, William Henry Irvine, who is reported to have been "a painter in the west" around 1892 (*Portrait and Biographical Record of Winnebago and Boone Counties, Illinois*, p. 426). The 1860 *Federal Census of Ogle County, Illinois* lists "Henry" as being eight years old and in school, nine years younger than his elder brother, Wilson Irvine's father. The *Rockford City Directory* of 1880 lists "Henry Irvine" as living with his father and he is still at that address in 1887-88 under his full name, "Wm. Henry Irvine," and identified as a painter. After 1892 he is no longer listed there, presumably having moved to "the west." To date, unfortunately, no further information about this artist uncle has been found.

18. Cheryl Cibulka Gordon, *Explorations of an American Impressionist: The Art of Wilson Irvine 1869-1936* (Exh. cat., Adams Davidson Galleries, Washington, D.C., The Bruce Museum, Greenwich, Connecticut, 1990) 10, 60. *The National Cyclopedia of American Biography*, XLII, p. 358, states that he attended evening classes at The Art Institute of Chicago for twenty years!

19. *Circular of Instruction...with a Catalogue of Students for 1895-96* (Chicago: The Art Institute of Chicago, 1896) 68; ... *for 1898-99* (1899) 175; ... *for 1899-1900* (1900) 32, 186; *School of Drawing, Painting... 1899-1900, with Catalogue of Students* (Chicago: The Art Institute of Chicago, 1900) 31, 175; *School of Drawing, Painting... Circular of Instruction for 1901-1902...* (Chicago: The Art Institute of Chicago, 1902) 31, 147; and ... *for 1902-1903* (1903) 33, 160. Also Registration Cards, 1900-1903. The author is indebted to Colleen Becker and Althea H. Huber of the archives staff, The Art Institute of Chicago, for their assistance in locating this information. There seems to be no record of Irvine's enrollment prior to the listings in the above documents.

20. The Irvines had two sons and a daughter, all born before 1900: Edwin Weyher (Ted), the eldest; Lois Madeleine (Simpson); and Jan Stuart, the youngest. Both sons served in the U.S. Army during World War I. Jan Irvine's daughter, Lydia Irvine (Macdonald) and son, Joseph P. Irvine, as well as Mrs. Wilson Irvine's niece, Evelyn Weyher Walker, have been very helpful to the author.

21. *Chicago Portrait Company: Its Book* (Chicago, 1905) 56.

22. *National Cyclopedia of American Biography*, XLII, p. 359.

23. *Chicago Portrait Company: Its Book*, pp. 167-169.

24. *Catalogue of the Salon de Refuse...At the Galleries of The Palette and Chisel Club. Atheneum Building, Chicago, Illinois, February 12, 1898, One Night Only*, cat. no. 22. The cover also bore the legend: "Special Permit from City Garbage Inspector."

25. N.P. Steinberg, "Art is Not Too Long: The Palette & Chisel Club Notes an Anniversary," *The Chicagoan* (April 1935) 33-36. Frank Holme, a newspaper artist (*Chicago Evening Post*), was the primary force behind many of the club's high jinks and comic productions. Irvine was among those who often assisted him.

26. *Chronicle* [Chicago], January 18, 1897. The article is accompanied by a drawing by Frank Holme which shows the club members — including Wilson Irvine — working diligently from a clothed model. The article indicates that the club at first rented the studio of Arnold Bunch (one of the founding members) for the Sunday sessions, sharing the rent and the expense of the models. By 1897 they were renting Room 428 in the Atheneum Building on Van Buren Street near Wabash Avenue. The move into Lorado Taft's studio is reported in Steinberg, *op. cit.*, p. 33.

27. From an undated clipping, "The Palette and Chisel Club," apparently from *The Inland Printer* [Chicago, ca. 1898], in the archives of the Palette and Chisel Club. In a listing of the club's members Irvine is identified as a portrait painter.

28. Peter Falk and Andrea A. Bien, Editors, *The Annual Exhibition Record of The Art Institute of Chicago 1888-1950* (Chicago: Sound View Press, 1990) 469-471.

29. William Wendt and Marion Wachtel both studied at The Art Institute of Chicago, the former in evening classes. Wendt exhibited California paintings (from his trips there in 1894 and 1896) at The Art Institute of Chicago following an 1898 trip to Cornwall with George Symons, a Chicago-born painter, who had also studied at that institution, and had first visited California in 1884 and again with Wendt in 1896. Irvine may have known both Wendt and Symons (Irvine, *Journal*, 1923, entries for March 24 and April 2). A painting in a photograph of William and Julia Wendt makes an interesting comparison with Irvine's *Birches*: see Patricia Trenton and William H. Gerdts, *California Light 1900-1930* (Exh. cat., Laguna Art Museum, 1990) 62. Payne did not visit California until 1911, but was a member of the Palette and Chisel Club, and a fellow exhibitor with Irvine and other members in 1913 at The Art Institute of Chicago. The relationships between Irvine and the California (and New Mexico) painters have yet to be explored.

30. This is akin to what William H. Gerdts has called "the glare aesthetic." See Gerdts, *American Impressionism* (Exh. cat., Seattle: The Henry Art Gallery, The University of Washington, 1980) 17-19; also Gerdts, "To Light the Landscape," *California Light 1900-1930*, pp. 19-22, especially p. 21.

31. A pencil drawing in one of Irvine's sketchbooks relates to this painting. It is executed from nearly the same vantage point as the view in *Dawn*, but, unlike the canvas, it is a vertical format. In so changing the axial orientation, the artist has created for the painting a more complex composition.

32. *Cf.* Monet's *A Morning on the Seine*, ca. 1897 (The Art Institute of Chicago); *A Branch of the Seine Near Giverny*, 1897 (Galerie du Jeu de Paume, Musée du Louvre, Paris); *Branch of the Seine Near Giverny II*, 1897 (Museum of Fine Arts, Boston); *The Seine at Giverny*, 1897 (National Gallery of Art, Washington, D.C.); *Morning on the Seine: Rain*, 1898 (National Museum of Western Art, Tokyo).

33. The official French government display did not include impressionist works. A loan exhibition gathered from private holdings in the United States featured works by Manet, Monet, Pissarro, Renoir, and Sisley. In the American section of the art palace one could see works by Julian Alden Weir, Childe Hassam, John Twachtman, Willard Metcalf, Robert Vonnoh (later a close friend of Irvine), and numerous others.

34. See Henry Regnery, *The Cliff Dwellers: A History of a Chicago Cultural Institution* (Chicago: Chicago Historical Bookworks, 1990). The Cliff Dwellers was originally called The Attic Club when it was founded in June of 1907, but the name was changed to The Cliff Dwellers at the organizational meeting on November 6 of that year. The Cliff Dwellers grew out of an earlier group called The Little Room, which met initially at the studio of Bessie Potter (who married Robert Vonnoh in 1899) and later at Ralph Clarkson's studio, both in the Fine Arts Building, usually on Friday afternoons, to discuss art, literature, and theater. Garland was a prime mover in all these ventures and Wilson Irvine was a member of both The Little Room and the Cliff Dwellers. The Cliff Dwellers' membership included a distinguished group of individuals: Hamlin Garland (Pulitzer Prize, 1922), sculptor Lorado Taft (Garland's brother-in-law), Chicago Symphony conductor Frederick A. Stock, writer Booth Tarkington (Pulitzer Prizes, 1919, 1922), journalist William Allen White (Pulitzer Prize, 1923), banker and patron of the arts Charles L. Hutchinson, physicist Robert Millikan (Nobel Laureate, 1923), and architect Louis Sullivan, among many other noted individuals. The guest list over the years is likewise impressive: Arnold Bennett, John Galsworthy, Theodore Dreiser, Padraic Colum, George Santayana, Fritz Kreisler, Victor Horta, Ralph Adams Cram, Lady Gregory and the Irish Players, to name a few. In January of 1909 the club moved into a penthouse atop Orchestra Hall. They dubbed it "The Khiva" to reflect the Southwestern origin of their name. The club is still active today but was recently forced out of its old quarters and now occupies space next door, overlooking its former home. After over three-quarters of a century, in 1984, women were finally admitted as full-fledged members.

35. Hamlin Garland, *Crumbling Idols* (Chicago and Cambridge: Stone and Kimball, 1894) 121-141.

36. Regnery, *op. cit., passim*; *The Cliff Dwellers Yearbook[s]*, 1911, 1914-15, 1915-16, 1916-17, 1917-18, 1918-19, *passim*.

37. Hamlin Garland, *A Son of the Middle Border* (New York: Macmillan, 1917) 457.

38. Garland, *Crumbling Idols*, 122-124.

39. See Adolph Robert Shulz, "The Story of the Brown County Art Colony," *Indiana Magazine of History*, XXXI, 4 (December 1935), 282-289; Josephine A. Graf, "The Brown County Art Colony," *Indiana Magazine of History*, XXXV, 4 (December 1939) 365-370; Barbara Judd and M. Joanne Nesbit, Editors, *Brown County's Art Colony: The Early Years* (Nashville, Indiana: Nana's Books, 1993) 22-28. See also William H. Gerdts, *Art Across America: Two Centuries of Regional Painting in America, 1710-1920* (New York: Abbeville Press, 1990) II, 261-272; Lyn Letsinger Miller, *The Artists of Brown County* (Bloomington: Indiana University Press, 1994). Also Gerdts, *Theodore Clement Steele: An American Master of Light* (Exh. cat., Evansville Museum of Arts & Science, Evansville, Indiana: Chameleon Books, New York, 1995).

40. Ray Mathis, *A Brown County History* (Bloomington, Indiana, 1936) 69. Reprinted 1993.

41. Shulz, *op.cit.*, p. 284.

42. Gordon, *op.cit.*, p. 10. M.Joanne Nesbitt and Barbara Judd, *Those Brown County Artists* (Nashville, Indiana: Nana's Books, 1993) 127.

43. An important Indianapolis periodical, *Modern Art*, began publication in 1893, the year of the exposition, and was the vehicle for some of the earliest American essays on impressionism. See Theodore C. Steele, "Impressionalism," *Modern Art*, I, 1 (Winter, 1893) unpaginated; and Otto Stark, "The Evolution of Impressionism," *Modern Art*, III,2 (Spring, 1895) 53-56. Stark, like Steele, was a prominent figure in the Hoosier group of painters.

44. See "A Critical Triumvirate," *Impressions on Impressionism* (Chicago: Central Art Association, 1894), probably written by Garland; William H. Gerdts, *American Impressionism* (1980) 103-105.

45. Gerdts, *Theodore Clement Steele…*, p. 78.

46. This outing seat was later manufactured by the Comfort Manufacturing Company, obviously a family business, since the address on the letterhead matches Irvine's own at the time: 2657 W.15th St., Chicago. Irvine's eldest son appears to have been one of the executives. An ink drawing on the letterhead depicts a young woman sitting in the outing seat [Fig. 8]. The style of the drawing is close to that on an announcement of an exhibition of Irvine's works at the Palette and Chisel Club in 1914 [Fig.10]. It is possible that Irvine was responsible for the drawings on both letterhead and announcement.

47. Letter from Col. G.L.Anderson, War Department, Board of Ordnance and Fortifications, dated August 23, 1917, to Wilson Irving [sic], Lyme, Connecticut. Private Archives.

48. Private Archives. The sketchbook also contains the Pittsburgh notes and some sketches that relate to his 1908 trip to France. Since Irvine was not in the habit of dating drawings in his sketchbooks, any more than he was his paintings, and since he could have used one sketchbook off and on for more than one year, the dating of this sketchbook is difficult; but, given the Breton subjects, it seems likely that he began using it as early as around 1908. In the records of his entries in exhibitions at The Art Institute of Chicago, the first title unquestionably of a Maine subject — *Camden Hills* — appears in 1908 and one of the drawings in this sketchbook is of Manana Island, done from Monhegan. He seems to have been on Monhegan more than once, however. This sketchbook also contains notes and sketches relating to his outing seat, patented in 1911. His address, written on an end page, is the one first listed in 1910 in the records of his entries in exhibitions at The Art Institute of Chicago.

49. Steinberg, *op.cit.*, p.35.

50. Irvine, *Diary*, 1888, entries July 6-7.

51. "Palette Scrapings," *The Cow Bell*, II, 6 (June 1, 1913). *The Cow Bell* was a monthly publication of the Palette and Chisel Club, beginning in 1912.

52. The author is indebted to Joel S. Dryer, Director of the Illinois Historical Art Project and its archives for the information concerning Irvine's involvement with these Chicago organizations. There is extensive documentation of the operations of the Chicago Commission for the Encouragement of Local Art in the Archives, Ryerson Library, The Art Institute of Chicago.

53. "News of the Art World," *Chicago Evening Post*, December 12, 1916.

54. *Chicago Evening Post*, December 17, 1918.

55. Letter, with "Painter Friends" letterhead, dated March 11, 1917, from Wilson Irvine to Victor Higgins, Secretary, Commission for the Encouragement of Local Art. The artists cited are listed with their addresses on the letterhead. C.E.L.A. Papers, Ryerson Library, The Art Institute of Chicago.

56. Town records, Lyme, Connecticut, show that Irvine acquired the Hamburg property on May 17, 1918. Letters addressed to the Irvines from their eldest son, Edwin (Ted), during the summer of 1917, were sent "c/o Mrs. J.W. Martin." They may have been boarding with her prior to finding a residence of their own. Records show that Martin property bordered on the place Irvine purchased in 1918.

57. *Bulletin of The Art Institute of Chicago*, X, 8 (December 1916) 234.

58. Unidentified clipping from an exhibition catalogue, which reproduces a letter from Wilson Irvine, indicating that his painting, *Approaching Storm*, (28" x 36", and No. 52 in the exhibition) was painted on Monhegan during the summer of 1914. Archives, Illinois Historical Art Project.

59. Jeffrey W. Andersen, *op.cit.*, pp. 134-135.

60. "News of the Art World," *Chicago Evening Post*, December 17, 1918. Review of Irvine's exhibition at O'Brien's gallery on South Michigan Boulevard. The review went on to say that "now partitions have been knocked out and great windows put in since the papers have been signed and the purchase money paid." Work on the house and studio, therefore, must have begun as soon as the property was purchased.

61. Unless otherwise noted, the information concerning this trip is taken from Wilson Irvine, *Journal*, 1923. Private Archives.

62. See Theodore J. Keane, *Friendly Libels* (Chicago: The Cliff Dwellers, 1924) 9, 22. Keane, a dean at the School of The Art Institute of Chicago, and to some of the younger and merrier element "the keen

dean," honored Irvine with two pencil portraits in this volume. Between 1916 and 1922 Keane had sketched portraits of many of his fellow Cliff Dwellers which were reproduced in the above publication. In the second portrait of Irvine he is looking down with squinting intensity at a black rook and a white pawn. Judging from Irvine's entries in his journals, he was a serious chess player. This passion may have been a legacy from his father who was reported to have been "a great chess player" who "spent many an hour with personal G.A.R. friends, solving the intricacies of the game." Obituary, Edwin A. Irvine, *The Rockford Morning Star*, December 2, 1911.

63. Irvine, *Journal*, February 14, 1923. Private Archives.

64. See letter from his eldest son, Ted, postmarked "Chicago, Ill., July 20, 1917," addressed to Irvine at Hamburg, c/o Mrs. J.W. Martin. Archives, Florence Griswold Museum. Also Irvine, *Journal*, 1929, entry for March 29.

65. Irvine, *Journal*, May 13, 1923.

66. Arthur G. Bradley, *Highways and Byways in North Wales* (London: Macmillan and Co., Ltd.,1909) 231-232. A pen and ink illustration by Joseph Pennell (p. 232) depicts the same bridge Irvine painted, but from another angle.

67. Irvine believed Callanish to be a Druid ceremonial site. In this he was accepting current lore, but, in fact, the stones are earlier, probably dating to between 2600 and 2000 B.C. The alignment of the stones seems to bear some relation to lunar and solar phenomena. See Aubrey Burl, *From Carnac to Callanish: The Prehistoric Stone Rows and Avenues of Britain, Ireland and Brittany* (New Haven and London: Yale University Press, 1993).

68. Irvine, *Journal*, August 26, 1923.

69. *Ibid.*, August 30. A journal for this 1908 trip abroad, if it exists, has yet to be found. Given the journals of 1888, 1923, and 1929, it seems reasonable to assume that he would have kept one on his first trip to Europe.

70. Although Pont-Aven is popularly associated with Gauguin and his circle, off and on during the last half of 1880s and mid-1890s, it was also a favorite area for American artists who began flocking there as early as 1866. See David Sellin, *Americans in Brittany and Normandy 1860-1910* (Exh. cat., Phoenix Art Museum, 1982) 13, and *passim*.

71. At the time of Irvine's visit, the painting collection now housed in the Museo di Capodimonte was displayed in what is now the archaeological Museo Nazionale.

72. Letter from Eckhart to Irvine, dated January 17, 1924. Private Archives.

73. Florence Davies, *op. cit.*

74. "Irvine Seen in New Guise in Carson Show," *Chicago Herald Examiner*, April 13, 1924.

75. *Christian Science Monitor*, August 7, 1924. Archives of American Art, Microfilm Reel 1233, Frame 163.

76. Exchange of correspondence between Rockford Art Asociation and Wilson Irvine, December 6, 1924. Archives, Rockford Art Museum.

77. *Atlanta Constitution*, May 10, 1925. Photograph shows Irvine in the company of several artists, including Ivan Olinsky, Wayman Adams, Edmund Greacen, and others.

78. A snapshot of a harbor scene at Martigues, stained with paint around the edges, obviously held by the artist while working, is surely the basis for one of his compositions (Private Collection). There are some changes in scale between photograph and painting, particularly in the boat that dominates the left foreground, and the distance between it and the landing and moored boats opposite, but the general composition is the same. The photograph is in private archives.

79. A cracked and paint-stained snapshot of two stalls of a stable with a horse looking out at the left over the head of a seated stable hand and a rooster standing in an open stall at the right is in private archives. An album on Irvine in the same archives contains a photograph of a signed painting that nearly duplicates the photograph. An etching by Irvine using the same composition, but reversed, is in the same album. A print of the etching is reproduced in Gordon, *op. cit*, p. 37. The scene may be from Charleston, South Carolina, and date ca. 1932.

80. Letter from Irvine to his son, Jan, posted at Lyme on February 18, 1926. Also see letter from Mrs. Irvine to Jan and his wife, written on January 1, 1926, indicating that her husband was painting snow scenes. Archives, Florence Griswold Museum.

81. Letter dated Lyme, January 20, 1926. Archives, Florence Griswold Museum.

82. Communications from National Academy of Design, dated April 15, 1926, and December 22, 1926, both signed by Charles C. Curran, Secretary. Private Archives.

83. The painting, now in a private collection, includes a number of figures in antebellum costume. Several sketches, possibly the initial studies for these figures, were done on stationery of the Salmagundi Club. Private Archives.

84. Letter from Mrs. Irvine to Jan and his wife, Josephine, dated May 22, 1926, while the Irvines were staying at a country inn near Richmond, Virginia. Also letter from Wilson Irvine to Jan, dated October 19, 1926, mailed from Lyme, reporting a lovely time in Vermont. Archives, Florence Griswold Museum.

85. *An Exhibition of Important Paintings by Prominent American Artists*, The Public Library, Joliet, Illinois, March 23-April 3 [1927].

86. A brown monotype landscape [Cat. no. 11] signed in pencil "Wilson Irvine" and dated "2-1-'13" is in a private collection.

87. *The Item Tribune*, New Orleans, February 5, 1928, p. 12.

88. *Ibid.*

89. Several artists with Chicago connections became members of the Taos-Santa Fe group in the early twentieth century, among them Ernest Martin Hennings, who had been a student at The Art Institute of Chicago. Others were Oscar Berninghaus, Gustave Baumann, Walter Ufer, and Victor Higgins. Hennings, Baumann, Ufer, and Higgins were all members of the Palette and Chisel Club. Baumann and Higgins were members of the Cliff Dwellers, Higgins had served with Irvine on Chicago's Commission for the Encouragement of Local Art, and Berninghaus was referred to as "your friend Berninghaus" in a note to Irvine from The Art Institute of Chicago in 1913. Ufer exhibited at Grand Central Galleries at the same time as Irvine's prismatic paintings were shown in 1930. Irvine's relationships with these artists have yet to be clarified.

90. Irvine identified the Leonardo as *Annunciation*, but he was probably referring to *The Virgin of the Rocks*.

91. In this respect Irvine parallels the French artist, Pierre Bonnard, who, around the beginning of the First World War, began to question his interest in impressionism and the direction it had taken him. He began to draw more and to emphasize composition. See James Thrall Soby, James Elliott, and Monroe Wheeler, *Bonnard and His Environment* (Ex. cat., Museum of Modern Art, in collaboration with The Los Angeles County Museum of Art, and The Art Institute of Chicago, 1964) 24.

92. Michael Quick, "Technique and Theory: The Evolution of George Bellows's Painting Style," *The Paintings of George Bellows* (New York: Harry N. Abrams, Inc., 1992) 9-95. Harold Spencer, "Criehaven, A Bellows Pastoral," *Bulletin* (Storrs, Connecticut: The William Benton Museum of Art, 1977) 18-38. See also Quick, *op. cit.*, pp. 24, 58.

93. Edward Alden Jewell, "The Summer Art Season Maintains Its Zestful Stride," *The New York Times*, August 4, 1929.

94. "Lyme Art Association," *The Christian Science Monitor*, August 5, 1929.

95. Alice Lawton, "Lyme Colony at Work and Play — Annual Summer Exhibition Now Open," *Boston Sunday Post*, July 28, 1929.

96. The author is informed by Mrs. Evelyn Weyher Walker, niece of Mrs. Wilson Irvine, that on a visit to Hamburg in 1931 she saw prismatic paintings in the studio and that Irvine explained them to her. She also stated that Irvine's daughter, Lois, had told her that it was she who called her father's attention to the prismatic effect when she was playing with a prism at about the age of ten or twelve. This would have been somewhere around 1910. If this is true, Irvine did not immediately commence his experiments with the prism, but how long it actually was before he began is still uncertain.

97. The most consistent pattern, when looking at objects through the prism, is one in which the dominant red and green halos appear on opposite sides of the same object, whether it is light or dark, or is against a light or dark background. In some instances, with light objects against light backgrounds under bright light, a fuller spectrum appears on each side. Thus, in snow under bright sunlight, a full "rainbow" of color appears on the edges of objects out-of-doors.

98. Unidentified newspaper clipping, "Artist Tells of Hebrides; Warns Against Stagnation in Landscape Painters' Life and Work." Review of exhibition at Carper Galleries, Detroit, 1924. Cited in Gordon, *op. cit.*, p. 27.

99. *Chicago Evening Post*, April 15, 1924. Archives of American Art, Reel 1233, Frame 165.

100. "Peace of New England Life Seen in Lyme Exhibition," *New York Tribune*, Sunday, August 13, 1922.

101. Irvine's stated interest in the ratio of 2 to 3 is applied here: the wall at the right edge of the painting begins 2/5ths of the distance up from the bottom of the painting and ends at the left edge 2/5ths of the distance down from the top. The masses of evergreen foliage to the right and left of the opening to the field beyond occupy roughly the 2/5ths sections of the upper corners, adding to the implied symmetry. This is further augmented by the curious parallelism of the two wavy saplings, like sled tracks lifted from the snow, near the center of the opening. For all its convincing on-the-spot immediacy, it is a carefully orchestrated composition.

102. "Art Exhibition at Old Lyme," *Shoreline Times* [Guilford, Connecticut], August 11, 1932.

103. Edward Alden Jewell, "Style and Technique," *The New York Times*, August 5, 1934.

104. Archives of American Art, Reel 1233, Frames 112-114, Wilson Irvine papers, 1913-1942. Gift of Lois Irvine Simpson, Oak Park, Illinois, 1977.

105. *Memories of Old Lyme Art Colony* 1900-1935 (Exh. cat., New York: Grand Central Art Galleries, Inc., March 28-April 15, 1967). From Introduction by Erwin S. Barrie, Director and Manager.

106. Lois Irvine Simpson, notes concerning her father's career. Private Archives.

CHRONOLOGY

1869   February 28, Wilson Henry Irvine born to
        Malinda (Underwood) and Edwin A. Irvine,
        near Byron, Illinois.

        Attends public school in Byron.

1885   Said to have worked as newspaper reporter
        from around this time to around 1888.
        Unconfirmed.

1888   January 2, working with airbrush.

        January 3, working on a landscape.

        June 22, graduates from Central High
        School, Rockford, Illinois.
        (Reported to have attended Jennings
        Seminary, Aurora, Illinois. Unconfirmed
        and doubtful.)

        July 16, arrives in Chicago, following day
        enrolls in a business school learning
        shorthand.

        August 11, visits The Art Institute of Chicago.

1891   Working as airbrush artist in Chicago.

        April 8, marries Lydia Weyher, of Lafayette,
        Indiana.

1893   May to November, World's Columbian
        Exposition held in Chicago.
        Around this time Irvine begins employment
        with Chicago Portrait Company, founded
        this year.

1895   Enrolls in evening life class at The Art
        Institute of Chicago, taught by Charles E.
        Boutwood. Continues in this class until 1902.

        November 1, together with other students
        in evening classes at The Art Institute of
        Chicago, establishes the Palette and Chisel
        Club.

1898   Treasurer, Palette and Chisel Club.

        February 12, participates in comic exhibition
        at Palette and Chisel Club.

1899   President, Palette and Chisel Club.

1900   Exhibits in Chicago and Vicinity show at The
        Art Institute of Chicago.

1902   Enrolls in evening illustration class at The
        Art Institute of Chicago, taught by Walter M.
        Clute. Continues in this class until 1903.

        Exhibits in first public exhibition of Palette
        and Chisel Club, Marshall Fields galleries,
        Chicago.

1903   Exhibits in Annual Exhibition of American
        Paintings and Sculpture, and in Chicago
        and Vicinity show, both at The Art Institute
        of Chicago.

        First Prize in Palette and Chisel Club
        Exhibition.

1904   Exhibits in Chicago and Vicinity show at
        The Art Institute of Chicago.

1905   Exhibits in Chicago and Vicinity show at
        The Art Institute of Chicago.

        November 6, the Cliff Dwellers club
        organized by Hamlin Garland.
        Irvine a founding member.

1906   Exhibits in Chicago and Vicinity show at
        The Art Institute of Chicago.
        First showing of New England subjects.

1907   Exhibits in Chicago and Vicinity show at The Art Institute of Chicago. Subjects from Gloucester, Massachusetts.

1908   Exhibits in Chicago and Vicinity show (subjects from Boston and Camden, Maine), and in Annual Exhibition of Watercolors by American Artists (subject from Camden), both at The Art Institute of Chicago.

Exhibits at Carnegie Institute Annual, Pittsburgh, Pennsylvania.

Travels to France. Paints in Brittany at Pont-Aven, Trémalo, Concarneau, and St. Malo.

1909   Exhibits in Annual Exhibition of American Paintings and Sculpture, in Chicago and Vicinity show, and in Annual Exhibition of Watercolors by American Artists, all at The Art Institute of Chicago.

Exhibits in Carnegie Institute annual, Pittsburgh, Pennsylvania, and in the Pennsylvania Academy of Fine Arts annual, Philadelphia.

1910   Exhibits in Chicago and Vicinity show, and in Annual Exhibition of Watercolors by American Artists, both at The Art Institute of Chicago.

Exhibits in Pennsylvania Academy of Fine Arts annual.

Serves on Art Committee, Cliff Dwellers.

1911   Exhibits in Chicago and Vicinity show (Municipal Art League Purchase Prize), and in Annual Exhibition of Watercolors by American Artists, both at The Art Institute of Chicago.

Exhibits in Carnegie Institute annual.

President, Chicago Society of Artists.

1912   Exhibits in Chicago and Vicinity show, and in Annual Exhibition of American Paintings and Sculpture (Martin B. Cahn Prize), both at The Art Institute of Chicago.

Exhibits in Corcoran Gallery of Art biennial, Washington, D.C.

1913   Invited by The Art Institute of Chicago to serve on the jury for the Annual Exhibition of Watercolors by American Artists.

Exhibits in Annual Exhibition of American Paintings and Sculpture, in Chicago and Vicinity show, and in Annual Exhibition of Watercolors by American Artists, all at The Art Institute of Chicago.

Exhibits in Pennsylvania Academy of Fine Arts annual.

1914   Exhibits in Annual Exhibition of American Paintings and Sculpture, in Chicago and Vicinity show, and in Annual Exhibition of Watercolors by American Artists, all at The Art Institute of Chicago.

Exhibits in Pennsylvania Academy of Fine Arts annual, and the Carnegie Institute annual.

Spends spring and summer months in east, painting in Connecticut and on Monhegan Island, Maine.

Exhibits in Lyme Art Association exhibition.

Solo exhibitions at Palette and Chisel Club, and Barrere Art Shop, Chicago.

1915   Exhibits in Annual Exhibition of American Paintings and Sculpture, and in Chicago and Vicinity show (Clyde M. Carr Prize), both at The Art Institute of Chicago.

Awarded Silver Medal at Panama-Pacific Exposition, San Francisco.

Exhibits in National Academy of Design winter exhibition, and at Toledo Museum of Art, Toledo, Ohio.

Serves on Board of Directors, Cliff Dwellers.

Spends summer painting in Connecticut.

Exhibits in Lyme Art Association annual.

1916   Exhibits in Annual Exhibition of American Paintings and Sculpture, and in Chicago and Vicinity show (Chicago Society of Artists Silver Medal, the Municipal Art League Prize, and the Palette and Chisel Club Prize), at The Art Institute of Chicago. Exhibits with Palette and Chisel Club at Society of Allied Arts, Peoria.

Exhibits in Corcoran Gallery of Art biennial, in the Pennsylvania Academy of Fine Arts annual, and at the Toledo Museum of Art.

Solo Exhibition at The Art Institute of Chicago.

Serves on Board of Directors, Cliff Dwellers.

Spends summer painting in Connecticut.

1917   Exhibits in Annual Exhibition of American Paintings and Sculpture, and in Chicago and Vicinity show (Mrs. William Frederick Grower Prize), both at The Art Institute of Chicago.

Exhibits in Pennsylvania Academy of Fine Arts annual, and National Academy of Design annual as well as its winter exhibition.

Spends summer painting in Connecticut.

1918   Spends summer painting in Connecticut and purchases home in Hamburg, Connecticut.

Exhibits in Annual Exhibition of American Paintings and Sculpture, and in Chicago and Vicinity show, both at The Art Institute of Chicago.

Solo exhibition at O'Brien's galleries, Chicago.

1919   Exhibits in Annual Exhibition of American Painting and Sculpture at The Art Institute of Chicago.

1920   Exhibits in Chicago and Vicinity show at The Art Institute of Chicago.

1921   Exhibits in Chicago and Vicinity show, and in Exhibition of the Friends of the Native Landscape, both at The Art Institute of Chicago.

Exhibits in Pennsylvania Academy of Fine Arts annual, and in National Academy of Design winter exhibition.

Awarded W. S. Eaton Purchase Prize at Lyme Art Association exhibition.

1922   Exhibits in Chicago and Vicinity show, and in Second Retrospective Exhibition of the Art Institute Alumni Association, both at The Art Institute of Chicago, and in National Academy of Design winter exhibition.

Solo exhibition at Carson, Pirie, Scott and Company galleries, Chicago.

1923   Spends over ten months abroad, painting at St. Ives, Zennor, and Clovelly on the Cornish coast in England, at Betwys-y-Coed in northern Wales, on the Island of Lewis in the Outer Hebrides, Scotland, and in Brittany, France, at Pont-Aven, Trémalo, and Concarneau. Visits London, Glasgow, Edinburgh, Paris, Giverny, Avignon, Carcassonne, Nîmes, Côte d'Azur, Marseille, Naples, Palermo, among other places.

Exhibits in Annual Exhibition of American Painting and Sculpture, and in Chicago and Vicinity show, both at The Art Institute of Chicago, and in the annual exhibition at the National Academy of Design.

1924   Exhibits in Annual Exhibition of American Painting and Sculpture at The Art Institute of Chicago, and in the National Academy of Design annual as well as its winter exhibition.

Exhibits in Lyme Art Association exhibition.

Two-man show with Gregory Smith at Rockford Art Association, Illinois.

Exhibits at Grand Rapids Art Gallery, Michigan.

With Guy Wiggins, exhibits at Carper Galleries in Detroit, Michigan.

Solo exhibition at Carson, Pirie, Scott and Company galleries.

1925   Exhibits Annual Exhibition of American Painting and Sculpture at The Art Institute of Chicago.

Exhibits in Atlanta, Georgia, with group from Grand Central Art Galleries.

Exhibits in National Academy of Design annual and in Pennsylvania Academy of Fine Arts annual.

Solo exhibition, Annex of Wadsworth Atheneum, Hartford, Connecticut.

May have visited Quebec, Canada during the summer this year, or the year previous.

1926   Elected Associate Member, National Academy of Design.

Exhibits Annual Exhibition of American Painting and Sculpture at The Art Institute of Chicago.

Exhibits in Corcoran Gallery of Art biennial, and National Academy of Design annual as well as its winter exhibition.

Painting at Westover, an 18th-century Georgian mansion on the James River, Virginia, in spring after traveling in Shenandoah Valley and Blue Ridge Mountains.

In Vermont in the fall.

1927   Exhibits aquaprints at Lyme Art Association, Milch Galleries in New York, Curtis H. Moyer galleries in Hartford, and Albert Roullier Galleries in Chicago.

Exhibits in National Academy of Design annual as well as its winter exhibition.

Exhibits in Carson, Pirie, Scott group exhibition at Public Library, Joliet, Illinois.

1928   Around January-February, painting in New Orleans.

Exhibits in National Academy of Design winter exhibition, and in The Founders' Exhibition at Grand Central Galleries.

Sails for France on December 21.

1929   Painting in France at Martigues, January 5 to February 5, and at Ronda, Spain, February 13 to March 15. Returns home by mid-April. In France, visits Paris and Marseille; in Spain, Madrid, Grenada, Toledo, and Segovia.

Exhibits in National Academy of Design winter exhibition and at Macbeth Galleries in New York.

Exhibits prismatic paintings at Lyme Art Association.

1930   Exhibits in National Academy of Design annual as well as its winter exhibition.

Solo exhibition, in March, of prismatic paintings at Grand Central Art Galleries.

Serves on Exhibition Committee and Library Committee, Lyme Art Association.

1931   Exhibits in National Academy of Design annual as well as its winter exhibition.

Serves on Library Committee of Lyme Art Association.

1932   Exhibits in National Academy of Design winter exhibition.

May have painted in Charleston, South Carolina, around this time.

1933   Exhibits in National Academy of Design annual.

1934   Exhibits in National Academy of Design annual.

Awarded Mr. and Mrs. William O. Goodman Prize at Lyme Art Association exhibition.

1935   Exhibits in National Academy of Design annual.

1936   Exhibits in National Academy of Design annual.

Dies at home of cerebral hemorrhage, August 21.

SELECTED BIBLIOGRAPHY

GENERAL (in chronological order):

Rockford City Directories. Rockford, Illinois, 1872-1901.

The History of Ogle County, Illinois. Chicago, H.F. Kett & Co., 1878.

Portrait and Biographical Record of Winnebago and Boone Counties, Illinois. Chicago, Biographical Publishing Co., 1892.

Garland, Hamlin. *Crumbling Idols: Twelve Essays on Art Dealing Chiefly with Literature, Painting and the Drama.* Chicago and Cambridge: Stone and Kimball, 1894.

Chicago Portrait Company: Its Book. Chicago, 1905.

Bradley, Arthur G. *Highways and Byways in North Wales.* London: Macmillan and Co., 1909.

Historical Encyclopedia of Illinois and History of Ogle County. Edited by Newton Bateman, Paul Selby, Horace G. and Rebecca H. Kauffman. Chicago, Munsell Publishing Co., 1909.

The Cliff Dwellers Yearbook[s], 1911-1919.

Catalogue: Rockford High Schools 1864-1914. Rockford, Illinois, 1914.

The National Cyclopedia of American Biography, XLII. New York, James T. White & Co., 1958.

Hoopes, Donelson F. *The American Impressionists.* New York: Watson-Guptill Publications, 1972.

Boyle, Richard J. *American Impressionism.* Boston: New York Graphic Society, 1974.

Bicentennial History of Ogle County. Ogle County Board, Ogle County, Illinois, 1976.

Gerdts, William H. *American Impressionism.* New York: Abbeville Press, 1984.

The Annual Exhibition Record of The Art Institute of Chicago 1888-1950. Edited by Peter Falk and Andrea A. Bien. Chicago: Sound View Press, 1990.

Regnery, Henry. *The Cliff Dwellers: A History of a Chicago Cultural Institution.* Chicago Historical Bookworks, 1990.

Gerdts, William H. *Art Across America: Two Centuries of Regional Painting in America, 1710-1920.* Vol.II. New York: Abbeville Press, 1990.

GENERAL EXHIBITION CATALOGUES (in chronological order):

Catalogue of the Twentieth Annual Exhibition of Water-Colors, Pastels and Miniatures by American Artists. Chicago: The Art Institute of Chicago, April 28-June 7, 1908.

Catalogue of the Twenty-first Annual Exhibition of Water-Colors, Pastels and Miniatures by American Artists. Chicago: The Art Institute of Chicago, May 11-June 13, 1909.

Sixteenth Annual Exhibition of the Society of Western Artists. Chicago: The Art Institute of Chicago, Mar. 5-18, 1912.

Catalogue of the Twenty-sixth Annual Exhibition of Water Colors, Pastels and Miniatures. Chicago: The Art Institute of Chicago, May 7-June 7, 1914.

Catalogue of a Special Exhibition of Paintings by Members of the Chicago Society of Artists. Chicago: The Art Institute of Chicago, June 11-21, 1914.
Seven Special Exhibitions...Exhibition of the Friends of Our Native Landscape. Chicago: The Art Institute of Chicago, Dec. 1921-Jan. 1922.

The Book and Catalogue of the Second Retrospective Exhibition of the Art Institute Alumni Association. Chicago: The Art Institute of Chicago, 1922.

National Academy of Design, 98th Annual Exhibition. New York: National Academy of Design, Mar. 17-Apr. 15, 1923. [Reproduces *Morning at the Pool.*]

National Academy of Design, Winter Exhibition. New York: National Academy of Design, Nov. 26-Dec. 20, 1932. [Reproduces *Lois and Betty-June.*]

Memories of the Old Lyme Art Colony 1900-1935. New York: Grand Central Art Galleries, 1967.

Corn, Wanda M. *The Color of Mood: American Tonalism 1880-1910.* San Francisco, M.H. DeYoung Memorial Museum and The California Palace of the Legion of Honor, 1972.

Bermingham, Peter. *American Painting in the Barbizon Mood.* Washington, D.C.: National Collection of Fine Arts, Smithsonian Institution, 1975.

Gerdts, William H. *American Impressionism.* Seattle, The Henry Art Gallery, The University of Washington, 1980.

Spencer, Harold, Susan Larkin and Jeffrey W. Andersen. *Connecticut and American Impressionism.* Storrs, Connecticut, The William Benton Museum of Art, The University of Connecticut, 1980.

Sellin, David. *Americans in Brittany and Normandy 1860-1910.* Phoenix, Arizona: Phoenix Art Museum, 1982.

Andersen, Jeffrey W., William H. Gerdts, and Helen A. Harrison. *En Plein Air: The Art Colonies at East Hampton and Old Lyme, 1880-1930.* Old Lyme, Connecticut, Florence Griswold Museum and East Hampton, New York, Guild Hall Museum, 1989.

Weinberg, H. Barbara, Doreen Bolger, David Park Curry, with the assistance of N. Mishoe Brennecke. *American Impressionism and Realism: The Painting of Modern Life, 1885-1915.* New York: The Metropolitan Museum of Art, 1994.

SOLO EXHIBITION CATALOGUES
(in chronological order):

Special Exhibition of Paintings by Mr. Wilson H. Irvine. Chicago: Barrere Art Shop, [1914].

Special Exhibitions...Paintings by Wilson Irvine. Chicago: The Art Institute of Chicago, Dec. 12, 1916-Jan. 2, 1917.

Recent Paintings by Wilson Irvine. Chicago: Carson, Pirie, Scott and Company Galleries, [1922].

The Galleries Announce an Exhibition of Recent Paintings of Wales, Cornwall and Brittany by Wilson Irvine. Chicago: Carson, Pirie, Scott and Company Galleries, [1924].

Exhibition of Paintings by Wilson Irvine. Hartford, Connecticut: Annex of Wadsworth Atheneum, November 16-30, 1925.

Exhibition of Aqua-Prints by Wilson Irvine, A.N.A. Hartford, Connecticut: Curtis H. Moyer, 1927.

Catalogue of an Exhibition of Original Aqua-Prints by Wilson Irvine, A.N.A. Foreword by Percy B. Eckhart. Chicago: Albert Roullier Art Galleries, 1927.

Exhibition of Prismatic Paintings by Wilson Irvine, A.N.A. New York: Grand Central Art Galleries, 1930.

Wilson Irvine. Chicago: Mongerson Galleries, June, 1983.

Wilson Henry Irvine, A.N.A. (1969-1936). Chicago: Campanile Galleries, [ca. 1983].

Gordon, Cheryl Cibulka. *Explorations of an American Impressionist: The Art of Wilson Irvine 1869-1936.* Washington, D.C.: Adams Davidson Galleries, 1990.

JOURNALS, PERIODICALS, NEWSPAPERS
(in chronological order):

"Will Irvine Married," *Rockford Republican,* April 9, 1891.

"Palette and Chisel Club," *Chronicle* [Chicago], January 18, 1897.

"Art," *Society,* I, 10 (December 6, 1912). [Review of 25th annual exhibition of American art at The Art Institute of Chicago. Reproduces *In Early Autumn.*]

"Palette Scrapings," *The Cow Bell,* II, 6 (June 1, 1913).

"At The Art Institute," *The Chicago Evening Post,* December 12, 1916.

"Mr. Irvine's Landscapes," *The Chicago Evening Post, December 17, 1918.* [Review of solo exhibition at O'Brien's galleries. *A Glimpse of the Sound* reproduced.]

"Mr. Irvine's Landscapes," *The Chicago Evening Post,* December 17, 1918. [Reproduces *A Glimpse of the Sound.*]

[Review of Lyme Art Association show, citing Irvine's Eaton Prize.] *The New York Times Book Review and Magazine,* August 14, 1921.

"Peace of Rural New England Life seen in Lyme Exhibition," *New York Tribune,* August 13, 1922.

"The Art Dealers," *The Chicago Evening Post,* February 22, 1922. [Review of solo exhibition at Carson, Pirie, Scott and Company galleries. *The Source* reproduced.]

Davies, Florence. "The Artist's Velvet Tie Gives Way to Hip Boots," *Detroit News,* March 16, 1924. [Review of joint exhibition with Guy Wiggins at Carper Galleries.]

"Irvine Seen in New Guise in Carson Show," *Chicago Herald Examiner,* April 13, 1924. [Review of solo exhibition at Carson, Pirie, Scott and Company Galleries.]

"New Pictures by Irvine," *The Chicago Evening Post,* April 15, 1924.

Cooke, Charles H. "Wilson Irvine Does Us Proud," *The Palette & Chisel,* May, 1924.

"At Old Lyme," *Christian Science Monitor,* August 7, 1924. [Reproduces *Cottage in England.*]

"Studio Windows," *The Hartford Daily Times,* November 14, 1925.

Cover [*The Broken Wall*], *The Literary Digest,* February 5, 1927.

"Wilson Irvine Invents the 'Aquaprint'," *The Art Digest,* October 1, 1927.

[Review of exhibition of aquaprints at Milch Galleries], *New York Herald Tribune,* October 20, 1927.

Eckhart, Percy B. "'Branching Tracery' by Wilson Irvine, A.N.A.," *The Union League Club Bulletin,* June 1928. [Cover features *Branching Tracery*].

Cary, Elisabeth Luther. "Founders' Exhibit Reveals Art Genuine Style," *The New York Times*, July 8, 1928.

Lawton, Alice. "Magic Carpet Leaving Daily From Old Lyme, Conn.," *Boston Evening Transcript*, July 28, 1928.

Eckhart, Percy B. "Quaint New England Scene Art Theme," T*he Union League Club Bulletin*, August 1928. [Cover features *The Old Homestead* (earlier title: *The Tillitson Place*)].

"An Eye for Art," *New Haven Register*, August 4, 1928.

Lawton, Alice. "Lyme Colony at Work and Play — Annual Summer Exhibition Now Open," *Boston Sunday Post*, July 28, 1929.

"The World of Art," *Providence Sunday Journal*, August 4, 1929.

Jewell, Edward Alden. "The Summer Season Maintains Its Zestful Stride," *The New York Times*, August 4, 1929.

"Lyme Art Association," *The Christian Science Monitor*, August 5, 1929.

Cover [*A Prismatic Winter Landscape*], *The Literary Digest*, January 31, 1931.

"Art Exhibition at Old Lyme," *Shoreline Times* [Guilford, Connecticut], August 11, 1932.

"Prismatic Motif Chance Discovery of Lyme Artist," *The Day* [New London, Connecticut], August 1, 1934.

Jewell, Edward Alden. "Style and Technique," *The New York Times*, August 5, 1934.

Shulz, Adolph Robert. "The Story of the Brown County Art Colony," *Indiana Magazine of History*, XXXI, 4 (December 1935), 282-289.

Obituary, *The New York Times*, August 23, 1936.

Sellroe, Edna. "Wilson Henry Irvine — Noted Landscape Painter — Beloved in Life — Revered in Memory by Art World," *Artistry: A Magazine Devoted to the Muses*, Oak Park, Illinois, June 1938.

ARCHIVAL SOURCES:
Irvine, Wilson H. *Diary*, 1888. Private Archives.

_____. *Journal*, 1923. Private Archives.

_____. *Journal*, 1929. Private Archives.

Irvine Family Archives.

Irvine Files: Archives of American Art (Microfilm Reel No. 1233), Florence Griswold Museum, The Art Institute of Chicago, Rockford Art Museum, Palette and Chisel Club.

Archives: Illinois Historical Art Project, Newberry Library (Chicago), Chicago Historical Society, Ryerson Library (The Art Institute of Chicago), Lyme Art Association.

Jensen, Susan. *Wilson Henry Irvine (1869-1936)*. Unpublished research paper, University of Denver, Colorado, 1995. Copy, Irvine Files, Florence Griswold Museum.

CATALOGUE

Dimensions in inches, height precedes width. Signature is "IRVINE", except when otherwise indicated. Since Irvine rarely dated his paintings the approximate dates given below are based upon collateral evidence of various kinds as well as subject and style. This is the first attempt to establish a working chronology of his paintings, so the approximate (ca.) dates should be considered tentative in most cases.

1. *Dawn* (1905)
   oil on canvas, 30 x 40 inches
   Signed and dated, lower right
   Courtesy of
   Cynthia and John W. Everets

2. *Birches* (1907)
   oil on canvas, 23 $3/8$ x 17 $3/8$ inches
   Signed and dated, lower right
   Private collection

3. *Houses of Breton* (1908)
   oil on canvas, 17 $1/2$ x 23 $3/8$ inches
   Signed and dated, lower right
   Private collection

4. *Evening in the Harbor* (ca. 1910)
   oil on canvas, 24 x 27 inches
   Signed, lower left
   Courtesy of
   Mr. and Mrs. Clement C. Moore

5. *Sea Sparkle* (ca. 1910)
   oil on canvas, 23 $1/4$ x 26 $3/8$ inches
   Signed, lower right
   Courtesy of Mr. and Mrs.
   George M. Yeager

6. *Sunrise* (ca. 1912)
   oil on canvas, 23 $3/8$ x 26 $1/2$ inches
   Courtesy of Mr. and Mrs.
   George M. Yeager

7. *Early Morning* (ca. 1912)
   oil on canvas, 28 $3/8$ x 35 $3/4$ inches
   Signed, lower left
   Courtesy of Mr. and Mrs.
   George M. Yeager

8. *Cool Shadows* (ca. 1913)
   oil on canvas, 29 x 36 inches
   Signed, lower left
   Courtesy of the Illinois Historical
   Art Project

9. *Grace of Spring* (ca. 1913)
   oil on canvas, 23 $1/2$ x 26 $1/4$ inches
   Signed, lower left
   Private collection

10. *Landscape, Lyme, Connecticut* (ca. 1913)
    oil on canvas, 30 x 32 $1/4$ inches
    Signed, lower right
    Courtesy of Smith College Museum of
    Art, Northampton, Massachusetts
    Bequest of Mrs. Lewis Larned Coburn

11. *Untitled Landscape* (1913)
    brown monotype, 5 $7/8$ x 7 $7/8$ inches
    Signed holograph "Wilson Irvine,"
    below right, and dated "2-1-'13"
    Courtesy of Harold and Editha
    Spencer

12. *Monhegan Bay, Maine* (ca. 1914)
    oil on canvas, 35 $3/8$ x 39 $1/2$ inches
    Signed, lower right
    Courtesy of Mr. and Mrs.
    George M. Yeager

13. *Abandoned* (ca. 1914)
    oil on canvas, 29 $1/2$ x 29 $3/8$ inches
    Signed, lower left
    Courtesy of Mr. and Mrs.
    George M. Yeager

14. *Evening Scene with Circus Wagons*
    (ca. 1915)
    oil on canvas, 23 $1/4$ x 26 $3/8$ inches
    Signed, lower right
    Private collection

15. *Untitled Landscape* (ca. 1915)
    color monotype, 11 $3/4$ x 14 $1/8$ inches
    Signed, lower left
    Private collection

16. *Meetinghouse Hill* (ca. 1916)
oil on canvas, 34 1/4 x 36 1/2 inches
Signed, lower left
Florence Griswold Museum
Gift of Mrs. Jan Irvine

17. *The Old Homestead* (ca. 1916)
oil on canvas, 35 1/2 x 46 1/2 inches
Signed, lower left
Courtesy of the Collection of the
Union League Club of Chicago

18. *Bridge, Old Lyme* (ca. 1916)
oil on canvas, 12 x 16 inches
Signed, lower left
Private collection

19. *Candlewood Ledge* (ca. 1916)
oil on canvas, 35 1/2 x 48 1/2 inches
Signed, lower right
Courtesy of Mr. and Mrs.
George M. Yeager

20. *Winter Light* (ca. 1918)
oil on canvas, 29 1/4 x 36 1/4 inches
Signed, lower right
Courtesy of Lydia Irvine Macdonald
and Stewart Macdonald

21. *Stone Wall At Old Lyme* (ca. 1918)
oil on canvas, 28 1/4 x 35 1/2 inches
Signed, lower right
Courtesy of Mr. and Mrs.
George M. Yeager

22. *Connecticut Landscape* (ca. 1920)
oil on canvas, 35 x 46 inches
Signed, lower left
Courtesy of the Wadsworth Atheneum,
Hartford, Connecticut
Gift of Mr. and Mrs.
Thomas L. Archibald

23. *Old Pastures* (ca. 1920)
oil on canvas, 35 x 46 inches
Signed, lower right
Courtesy of the Rockford Art Museum,
Rockford, Illinois

24. *Boats of St. Ives* (1923)
oil on canvas, 23 1/2 x 26 1/2 inches
Signed, lower right
Private collection

25. *St. Ives, Cornwall* (1923)
oil on canvas, 29 1/2 x 36 inches
Signed, lower left
Courtesy of the Geist Collection

26. *The Quay, St. Ives* (1923)
oil on canvas, 29 x 36 1/4 inches
Signed, lower right
Courtesy of Joseph P. Irvine,
Grandson of the Artist

27. *Pont Mawr, Llanrwst, Wales* (1923)
oil on canvas, 27 x 32 inches
Signed, lower right
Courtesy of Suzanne J. Harrington

28. *Harbor at Stornoway* (1923)
oil on canvas, 24 x 27 inches
Signed, lower right
Courtesy of Mrs. Marjorie Harshbarger,
Belfair, Washington

29. *The Carousel, Brittany* (1923)
oil on canvas, 25 x 30 inches
Signed, lower left
Courtesy of Kirsten Halston

30. *Rooftops* (1923)
oil on canvas, 23 1/2 x 26 1/2 inches
Signed, lower right
Private collection

31. *St. Ives, Cornwall* (1923)
oil on panel, 9 1/2 x 13 inches
Signed, lower left
Private collection

32. *Stream Drift* (ca. 1924)
oil on canvas, 24 3/4 x 29 1/2 inches
Signed, lower right
Courtesy of Mr. and Mrs.
George M. Yeager

33. *Cloud Shadows* (ca. 1926)
oil on canvas, 24 1/2 x 29 inches
Signed, lower left
Courtesy of Mr. and Mrs.
George M. Yeager

34. *The Broken Wall* (ca. 1926)
oil on canvas, 34 1/4 x 45 1/4 inches
Signed, lower left
Courtesy of Mr. and Mrs.
George M. Yeager

35. *Heavy Snow* (ca. 1926)
oil on canvas, 24 x 27 inches
Signed, lower right
Courtesy of Lydia Irvine Macdonald
and Stewart Macdonald

36. *Untitled Landscape* (ca 1927)
aquaprint on paper,
14 1/8 x 16 7/8 inches
Signed, lower left
Courtesy of Mr. and Mrs.
George M. Yeager

37. *Untitled Landscape* (ca 1927)
aquaprint on paper, 15 x 18 inches
Signed, lower left
Florence Griswold Museum
Gift of Mr. and Mrs. Joel S. Dryer,
the Illinois Historical Art Project

38.   *New Orleans Courtyard* (1927-28)
oil on canvas, 29 x 35 inches
Signed, lower left
Courtesy of Joseph P. Irvine,
Grandson of the Artist

39.   *Bird Seller, New Orleans* (1927-28)
oil on canvas, 11 1/2 x 15 1/2 inches
Signed, lower left
Private collection

40.   *Cal, The Widower* (ca. 1928)
oil on canvas, 30 x 40 inches
Signed, lower right
Courtesy of the Rockford Art
Museum, Rockford, Illinois
Gift of Mrs. Wilson Irvine

41.   *Spanish Town* (1929)
watercolor on paper,
11 7/8 x 12 3/4 inches
Signed, lower left
Private collection

42.   *The Marshes* (ca. 1929)
oil on canvas, 24 1/4 x 29 inches
Signed, lower left
Private collection

43.   *Still Life With Petunias* (ca. 1932)
oil on canvas, 23 1/2 x 27 inches
Signed, lower left
Private collection

44.   *Lady in Red* (ca. 1932)
oil on canvas, 24 1/2 x 28 1/2 inches
Signed, lower left
Courtesy of
Mr. and Mrs. Joseph Rhodes

45.   Sketchbooks
graphite on paper
Courtesy of Lydia Irvine Macdonald
and Stewart Macdonald

46.   *The Broken Wall,* cover,
The Literary Digest, February 5, 1927
Courtesy of the Library of the
National Museum of American Art
and the National Portrait Gallery,
Smithsonian Institution,
Washington, DC

ACKNOWLEDGMENTS

No project of this sort is possible without the cooperation and generosity of many individuals. During the course of my research for this exhibition I have been extremely fortunate in this regard.

I am especially indebted to the artist's granddaughter, Lydia Irvine Macdonald, and grandson, Joseph P. Irvine, as well as to George and Barbara Yeager, and to Joel S. Dryer, Director of the Illinois Historical Art Project. Without their help this exhibition and the accompanying catalogue could not have attained their proper form. It has been a pleasure to work with Jeffrey Andersen, Director of the Florence Griswold Museum, and with its Curator, Jack Becker, both of whom have given me their full cooperation throughout this project. Special thanks to the Registrar at the Florence Griswold Museum, Laurie Bradt.

Among those I wish to thank for their assistance and interest in this exhibition are John Molyneaux of the Rockford Public Library; Evelyn Walker, niece of Mrs. Wilson Irvine; Andy Penaluna of Swansea, Wales; Natalia J. Lonchyna, Senior Reference Librarian of the Ryerson and Burnham Libraries, The Art Institute of Chicago; Coleen Becker and Althea H. Huber of the Archives staff, The Art Institute of Chicago; Daniel Schulman, Assistant Curator, Kate Heston, Nick Barron, and the curatorial staff of The Art Institute of Chicago; Matthew Herbig, Curator of Collections, and the curatorial staff of the Rockford Art Museum; David Dearinger, Chief Curator of the National Academy of Design; Patricia Randle, Richard Morrow, and Frank Hensley of the Palette and Chisel Academy of Fine Arts, Chicago; Marc Middleton of the Cliff Dwellers, Chicago; the staff of the Newberry Library and Emily Clark of the Chicago Historical Society; Marianne Richter, Curator of the Union League Club of Chicago; Merja Lehtinen, Director of the Lyme Art Association; Linda Muelig of Smith College Museum of Art and its curatorial staff; Richard and Geraldine Love; Amy Henderson of the Terra Museum of American Art; Suzanne Harrington, Marjorie Harshbarger, Joan Bain Frangella, Sharlene Beech, and Phyllis Thompson; John and Cynthia Everets, Joseph and Lee Rhodes, Joseph and Gigi Rhodes, Kirsten Halston, The Geist Collection, Mr. and Mrs. Clement C. Moore, and Sally Bill; Jeffrey Cooley, The Cooley Gallery, Old Lyme; Thomas Kulina and Alan and Nancy Bernard; David Butler, Director, Sheldon Swope Art Museum, Terre Haute, Indiana; John W. Streetman III, Director, Evansville Museum of Arts and Science, Evansville, Indiana; Sheila Dugan, Maureen Callahan, and Meredith Maluchnik of Vose Galleries, Boston; Patricia Dryer and Suzanne Kaufman; Town Clerk's Office, Lyme, Connecticut; Susan E. Shockley of The Parthenon, Nashville, Tennessee; Susan Jenson, Robert J. Fisher, Henry Eckert, Lisa Warnstedt, Mark Murray, Michael M. Schwartz, Colleen Kollar Zorn, Lee Howard, Susan Desch, Barbara Judd, John W. Henry, and Carrie Wild; Andreas Fischer, Kevin B. Leonard, Michael Moser, and Richard Norton; Diane Schweier Krall of the Indianapolis Museum of Art; Erika Dowell of the Fine Arts Library, Indiana University; Eric L. Mundell of the Indiana Historical Society; Ankeney Weitz, Director, University Gallery, Denison University; Rayonia A. Babel, Aurora University Library; William F. Clemens, Aurora Historical Society; Nancy Anderson, Northern Illinois Library System Reference Services; Thomas Jacoby, Art & Design Librarian, and the Interlibrary Loan Department, Homer Babbidge Library, The University of Connecticut.

A special debt of thanks is owed to designer Tom Goddard for giving form to this catalogue.

As always, I am indebted to my wife, Editha Hayes Spencer, for her patience, interest, and support throughout the project, and for her critical eye and editorial skills. She is indispensable.

HAROLD SPENCER
Ashford, Connecticut, April, 1998

PLATE 1. *Early Morning* (ca. 1912)
oil on canvas, 28 $\frac{3}{8}$ x 35 $\frac{3}{4}$ inches
Signed, lower left
Courtesy of Mr. and Mrs. George M. Yeager

PLATE 2. *St. Ives, Cornwall* (1923)
oil on canvas, 29 1/2 x 36 inches
Signed, lower left
Courtesy of the Geist Collection

PLATE 3. *Boats of St. Ives* (1923)
oil on canvas, 23 1/2 x 26 1/2 inches
Signed, lower right
Private collection

PLATE 4. *Houses of Breton* (1908)
oil on canvas, 17 1/2 x 23 3/8 inches
Signed and dated, lower right
Private collection

PLATE 5. *The Old Homestead* (ca. 1916)
oil on canvas, 35 1/2 x 46 1/2 inches
Signed, lower left
Courtesy of the Collection of the
Union League Club of Chicago

PLATE 6. *Candlewood Ledge* (ca. 1916)
oil on canvas, 35 1/2 x 48 1/2 inches
Signed, lower right
Courtesy of Mr. and Mrs. George M. Yeager

PLATE 7. *Connecticut Landscape* (ca. 1920)
oil on canvas, 35 x 46 inches
Signed, lower left
Courtesy of the Wadsworth Atheneum, Hartford, Connecticut
Gift of Mr. and Mrs. Thomas L. Archibald

PLATE 8. *Stream Drift* (ca. 1924)
oil on canvas, 24 3/4 x 29 1/2 inches
Signed, lower right
Courtesy of Mr. and Mrs. George M. Yeager

PLATE 9. *The Carousel, Brittany* (1923)
oil on canvas, 25 x 30 inches
Signed, lower left
Courtesy of Kirsten Halston

PLATE 10. *Bird Seller, New Orleans* (1927-28)
oil on canvas, 11 1/2 x 15 1/2 inches
Signed, lower left
Private collection

PLATE 11. *Cool Shadows* (ca. 1913)
oil on canvas, 29 x 36 inches
Signed, lower left
Courtesy of the Illinois Historical Art Project

PLATE 12. *The Marshes* (ca. 1929)
oil on canvas, 24 1/4 x 29 inches
Signed, lower left
Private collection

PLATE 13. *Lady in Red* (ca. 1932)
oil on canvas, 24 1/2 x 28 1/2 inches
Signed, lower left
Courtesy of Mr. and Mrs. Joseph Rhodes

PLATE 14. *Still Life With Petunias* (ca. 1932)
oil on canvas, 23 ¹/₂ x 27 inches
Signed, lower left
Private collection

PLATE 15. *Meetinghouse Hill* (ca. 1916)
oil on canvas, 34 1/4 x 36 1/2 inches
Signed, lower left
Florence Griswold Museum
Gift of Mrs. Jan Irvine

PLATE 16. *Evening in the Harbor* (ca. 1910)
oil on canvas, 24 x 27 inches
Signed, lower left
Courtesy of Mr. and Mrs. Clement C. Moore

PLATE 17. *Dawn* (1905)
Oil on canvas, 30 x 40 inches
Signed and dated, lower right
Courtesy of Cynthia and John Everets

PLATE 18. *Monhegan Bay, Maine* (ca. 1914)
oil on canvas, 35 3/8 x 39 1/2 inches
Signed, lower right
Courtesy of Mr. and Mrs. George M. Yeager

PLATE 19. *Winter Light* (ca. 1918)
oil on canvas, 29 1/4 x 36 1/4 inches
Signed, lower right
Courtesy of Lydia Irvine Macdonald
and Stewart Macdonald

PLATE 20. *Stone Wall At Old Lyme* (ca. 1918)
oil on canvas, 28 1/4 x 35 1/2 inches
Signed, lower right
Courtesy of Mr. and Mrs. George M. Yeager

PLATE 21. *The Broken Wall* (ca. 1926)
oil on canvas, 34 1/4 x 45 1/4 inches
Signed, lower left
Courtesy of the Mr. and Mrs. George M. Yeager